craft **workshop**

# rags & remnants

craft **workshop**

# rags & remnants

Learn the traditional art of ragwork in 25 step-by-step projects

## Lizzie Reakes

photography by Tim Imrie

**southwater**

*For my late Dad — for all the*
*support and encouragement*
*he gave me*

This edition is published by Southwater

Southwater is an imprint of Anness Publishing Ltd
Hermes House, 88–89 Blackfriars Road, London SE1 8HA
tel. 020 7401 2077; fax 020 7633 9499
www.southwaterbooks.com; info@anness.com

© Anness Publishing Ltd 1996, 2006

UK agent: The Manning Partnership Ltd, 6 The Old Dairy,
Melcombe Road, Bath BA2 3LR; tel. 01225 478444;
fax 01225 478440; sales@manning-partnership.co.uk

UK distributor: Grantham Book Services Ltd,
Isaac Newton Way, Alma Park Industrial Estate, Grantham,
Lincs NG31 9SD; tel. 01476 541080; fax 01476 541061;
orders@gbs.tbs-ltd.co.uk

North American agent/distributor: National Book Network,
4501 Forbes Boulevard, Suite 200, Lanham, MD 20706;
tel. 301 459 3366; fax 301 429 5746; www.nbnbooks.com

Australian agent/distributor: Pan Macmillan Australia,
Level 18, St Martins Tower, 31 Market St, Sydney,
NSW 2000; tel. 1300 135 113; fax 1300 135 103;
customer.service@macmillan.com.au

New Zealand agent/distributor: David Bateman Ltd,
30 Tarndale Grove, Off Bush Road, Albany, Auckland;
tel. (09) 415 7664; fax (09) 415 8892

A CIP catalogue record for this book is available from the
British Library.

Publisher: Joanna Lorenz
Project Editor: Judith Simons
Photographer: Tim Imrie
Designer: Susannah Good
Stylist: Fanny Ward
Illustrators: Vana Haggerty and Madeleine David

Previously published as *New Crafts: Ragwork*

10 9 8 7 6 5 4 3 2 1

# CONTENTS

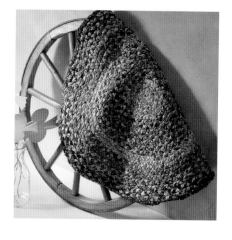

# INTRODUCTION

RAGWORK IS A TRADITIONAL CRAFT THAT ALL BUT DISAP-PEARED EARLIER THIS CENTURY BUT WHICH HAS RECENTLY BEEN REDISCOVERED AS A THRIVING NEW TEXTILE CRAFT. ITS GREAT APPEAL — ECONOMICALLY, ENVIRONMENTALLY AND CRE-ATIVELY — IS THAT IT USES RECYCLED MATERIALS, TRANSFORMING OLD, WORN FABRICS INTO PRACTICAL, USEFUL WORKS OF ART.

SIX DIFFERENT TECHNIQUES — HOOKING, PRODDING, PLAITING, KNITTING, CROCHET AND WRAPPING — ARE DESCRIBED IN THE BASIC TECHNIQUES SECTION, AND EXAMPLES OF EACH TECHNIQUE ARE THEN ILLUSTRATED IN THE SPECIALLY COMMISSIONED PRO-JECTS THAT FOLLOW. THE GALLERY SECTION SHOWS FURTHER EXAMPLES OF CONTEMPORARY ARTISTS' WORK TO INSPIRE YOU.

ENJOY THE MANY IDEAS AND PROJECTS ILLUSTRATED IN THIS BOOK, AND TURN YOUR RAGS INTO RICHES!

*Opposite: The step-by-step projects feature a wonderful range of ragwork items, including original designs for rugs, wall pieces, cushions and chair pads, mirror and picture frames, jewellery, and fashion and home accessories.*

# HISTORY OF RAGWORK

RAGWORK IS CURRENTLY ENJOYING IMMENSE POPULARITY, WITH A RESURGENCE OF INTEREST FROM BOTH MAKERS AND COLLECTORS. IT IS NOT UNCOMMON TO SEE HOOKED, PRODDED OR WRAPPED TEXTILES EXHIBITED ALONGSIDE CERAMICS, METALWORK AND JEWELLERY AT CRAFTS VENUES. THIS APPRECIATION AND ENTHUSIASM FOR RAGWORK AS A DECORATIVE APPLIED ART FORM IS A NEW RE-EVALUATION, AND A FAR CRY FROM THE CRAFT'S HUMBLE ORIGINS.

Modern ragwork derives from traditional rag rug making, which includes several related textile techniques, including hooking, prodding and plaiting. The history of rag rugs is necessarily somewhat sketchy – most rugs were made to be used underfoot, and were eventually discarded. Surviving examples show just how durable handmade rugs can be, often outlasting their makers. Collectors of rag rugs may not know many details about their origins, unless a particular rug has been carefully tended and handed down within a family from generation to generation.

There is much debate about the origins of the textile techniques used in rag rugs. Adapting textiles to make practical floor coverings to provide insulation and warmth is an idea that has evolved throughout history. Material has been manipulated in various ways to produce a surface pile, and weaving techniques have been used to produce flat rugs.

The hooking technique has been in use worldwide for centuries. The early Egyptians used a form of embroidery which left a looped surface. It is thought that the technique of hooking rugs came originally from Scandinavia. From there it was introduced to Britain, and later to the New World by the early settlers. Rug hooking became associated particularly with the east coast of America and the coastal provinces of Canada and Newfoundland. The designs of these rugs often reflect their proximity to the sea, incorporating shells, compasses, fish or an anchor. Makers met at rug hooking "bees", where they exchanged patterns and worked together on large projects.

The technique of prodded rugs, worked from the underside, flourished in England and Wales alongside hooking but never reached America. Some of these rugs were made in Canada and Newfoundland, where they were called "poked" mats.

Hooked and prodded rug designs were hand drawn on the hessian background, often using a charred stick as a marker. Early 19th-century rugs are typically decorated with simple motifs or patterns. Geometric designs probably made use of available shapes, using everyday household objects to serve as templates; straight lines and circles drawn round dinner plates were very common.

Fashions in interior decoration also influenced rug designs. Motifs were often copied from wallpaper, ceramics or the designs on carved furniture. Flowers were always popular and were often highly stylized, which added to the charm of the naïve pattern-making. More refined designs, in Britain and America, copied the more sophisticated ornament of expensive Aubusson rugs or Wilton and Axminster carpets, with flower heads placed neatly inside a scroll-like border.

At first, hooked rugs were almost uniform in shape and size – a rectangle of about 60 x 100 cm (24 x 40 in). This format was perfect for laying in pride of

*Left: Hand-hooked in woollen rags with a looped pile, this intricate design is reminiscent of ecclesiastical stained glass windows. The outlines of the roundels are further emphasized with embroidery work.*

*Above: Flowers were an ever-popular design
source. Here a zigzag border of repeat triangles
frames three flower heads intertwined in curved
branches bearing new buds.*
*114 x 201 cm (45 x 79 in); 1835.*

*Right: This design shows two horses parading one
behind the other. Above them hangs a stylized tree
branch bearing large flower heads. Made from
woollen rags, hand-hooked with a looped pile.*
*53 x 86 cm (21 x 34 in); date unknown.*

*Above: Another variation of the flower theme, here three rose heads are framed within a scalloped border. Made from woollen rags, hand-hooked with a looped pile.*
*99 x 124 cm (39 x 49 in); late 19th-century.*

place in front of the fire. Hearthrugs often had a half-moon, or semi-circular, format.

Another technique which developed in New England in the early 19th century was plaiting, or braiding. Strips of fabric were plaited, and then joined by stitching them together to form the rug's shape – usually circular, oval or rectangular. Different techniques were sometimes worked together within one rug; a favourite combination was to hook the centre picture and frame it with a simple plaited border.

Designs on rugs developed to feature domestic animals such as cats and dogs, or farmyard hens. Local buildings, landscapes and sea views all occur, depending on the locality. Text was also popular, especially commemorative dates or a simple greeting – this may be the origin of the "Welcome" mat. Certain characteristics determine the area where a rug had been made: for example, beavers and maple leaves often appear on Canadian hooked rugs.

Rag rug making reached the height of its popularity during the late 19th century and into the beginning of this century. It was always associated with working class culture, and was seen as a thrift craft practised by the poverty-stricken; to make a rug cost nothing but time. Long before recycling became an environmental concern, it was a way of life – a practical reality. Nothing went to waste.

Old clothes were handed down until they were no longer serviceable. The source material, the main ingredient of rug making, was worn garments. These were cut into long strips for hooking, or short clippings for prodding: normally a job for the children. Old sacking, made from woven jute cloth imported from India and used as packaging for grain or other foodstuffs, was recycled for the background fabric. Hooks and prodders were adapted from any suitable household tool, such as a wooden clothes peg or large masonry nail, sharpened into a pointed hook.

Many traditional rugs feature the small range of colour tones that were available in the clothing of the time. When chemical dyes became more commonplace, wool was often dyed in lots for the plainer background areas.

Rag rug making continued in popularity during the Second World War, but slumped soon after. This was partly due to technical developments within the carpet industry, which made domestic carpets widely affordable. This eventually led to the vogue for wall-to-wall broadloom carpeting. The craft of rug making still existed but it was no longer such a necessity. People wanted to forget past hardships and to celebrate a new beginning. Unfortunately, a rag rug

*Right: This checkerboard design, incorporating alternate diamond and stylized flower squares, was probably inspired by popular quilt designs of the period. Hand-hooked from woollen rags, with a looped pile.*
*264 x 150 cm (104 x 59 in); date unknown.*

symbolized poverty and many serviceable rugs were discarded.

The modern revival in ragwork is strongly associated with environmental concerns and the ways in which the maker can re-use so-called waste materials. The techniques are simple enough to encourage all abilities and age groups, including community groups. For beginners and professionals alike, the attraction of working with rags begins with the initial search for fabrics. What better place to start than at a jumble sale, where a kaleidoscope of colours is available at little cost? Sort them into colour lots, machine wash and cut into strips, and the fabric is ready for working.

As in the past, hooking designs are drawn out on a hessian background. Fabrics are then used like paint, to build up patterns and to fill in blocks of colour. Working with unlikely fabrics can lead to exciting results. Who would have thought that crimplene would be a sought-after fabric? There are constant surprises in

store when you are working with redundant materials, and part of the appeal is that the outcome is not absolutely controllable. The same fabric can vary enormously depending on which ragwork technique is used. Knitting and crochet produce beautiful, subtle tones when working with printed cottons. Lurex and nylon fabrics are transformed in wrapping or hooking, and old woollens are ideal for prodded ragwork. A modern approach is to blend in other materials, waste packaging such as plastic and foil, to give a multi-textured effect.

Contemporary ragwork is not simply concerned with producing floor rugs – there are a great many other possibilities. Modern textile artists work on different scales, employing various techniques to create smaller articles, such as jewellery, mirror frames and hats. The wealth of new fibres and fabrics available today helps to inspire the contemporary ragworker. Who knows what a typical rag rug from the late 1990s will look like in tomorrow's world?

# GALLERY

As we have seen, ragwork encompasses many different techniques. This gallery illustrates a selection of work by nine professional contemporary makers, each of whom has an approach that is totally unique. The examples of their work range from large floor rugs to thin rectangular banners, and they explore such diverse design themes as childhood memories and cake decoration. All the work is made from recycled fabric and materials. Each piece is totally different, reflecting the exciting developments being explored in ragwork today.

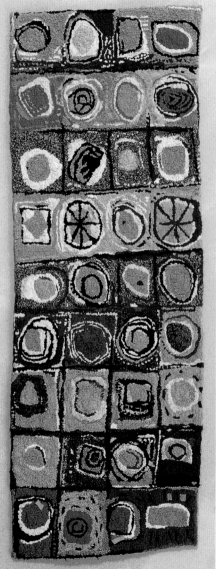

*Above:* UNTITLED
127 x 117 cm (50 x 46 in)
One of a pair of wall-hangings based on the theme of dance commissioned by Alnwick Playhouse. The figurative design has a strong feeling of movement, emphasized by the swirling skirt.

Woollen fabric strips have been hooked through to leave a loop pile surface, while areas of prodding in the skirt and towards the edges of the hanging provide longer texture.
*(By kind permission of Alnwick Playhouse.)*
ALI RHIND

*Right:* TATTOOS
160 x 56 cm (63 x 22 in)
This design was inspired by a book jacket from the early 1960s. The circle and star design is hooked in a variety of fabrics from towelling to crimplene, with a cut pile.
LIZZIE REAKES

*Left:* MYTHOLOGICAL BEAST

97 x 57 cm (38½ x 22½ in)
The beast symbolizes strength, power and vitality, combined with sensitivity and vulnerability. Many different fibres and fabrics have been hooked, including unspun fleece. The pile has been cut and sculpted, with mirror inlay. The wallhanging is finished with hand-felted pompoms and tassels.
*(By kind permission of Vale Royal Borough Council and Winsford Community Arts Centre)*
LYNNE STEIN

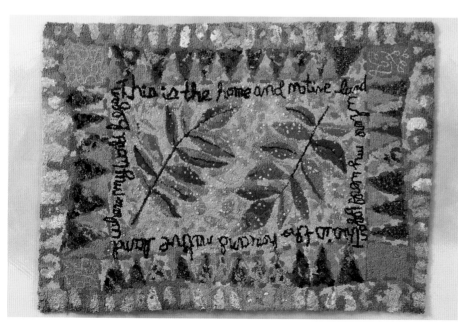

*Left:* THIS IS THE HOME AND NATIVE LAND WHERE MY WORLD BEGAN

100 x 160 cm (40 x 63 in)
The maker of this rug uses her native Canada as inspiration for much of her work. Autumnal colours depict images from a familiar landscape. The title's text is framed in a border of abstract triangles. A mixture of cast-off fabrics and plastic strips have been used in a cut and loop surface pile.
JU JU VAIL

*Below:* BATTENBURG
123 x 31 cm
(48½ x 12¼ in)
This hooked wall piece
blends a mixture of
fabrics, including
wool/acrylic, nylon, lycra
and cotton jersey, all with
a cut pile surface. Sequins
add extra interest. Pastel
shades and loose
checkerboard shapes are
combined in a painterly
fashion, and surmounted
by a crown.
LIZZIE REAKES

*Opposite:* DAISY, DAISY
100 cm (40 in) diameter
This multi-directional rug
was made with the
intention of exploring
surface texture for the
visually impaired. Plastics
and foils were hooked to a
higher pile height to
enhance the looped border
areas, petal outline shapes
and areas within the
flower. The rest of the rug
has a cut pile surface to
give textural contrast.
LIZZIE REAKES

*Above:* THE RED SLIPPER
46 x 30 cm (18 x 12 in)
Nostalgic memories are
the focal point for this
delightful and original
mixed media design. A
child's slipper, hooked in
rags, lies against a chintz
background encased in a
white weatherboard
house, with two miniature
hooked slippers suspended
from a line above.
SUSAN LINDSAY

*Above left:* RECYCLED HEADS
82 x 77 cm (32½ x 30½ in) and 100 x 120 cm (40 x 48 in)
These Greek-mosaic-style heads are made in denim, prodded through printed hessian sacking cloth with the text still visible. The features are enhanced by using darker denim against a faded denim background. The two pieces are reversible.
BEN HALL

*Left:* RECYCLED TOOLS
Smallest rug 150 x 80 cm (59 x 32 in)
This artist has used the theme of traditional domestic tools to make a set of prodded rugs in recycled denim. Dark indigo denim has been used to define the tool shapes and the background area is made from many pairs of worn, faded jeans.
BEN HALL

*Above:* FLOWER RUG
104 x 87 cm (41 x 34 in)
This design is hooked in five colours, using woollen and tweed fabrics, and has a loop pile surface throughout. The stylized flower motifs are set in contrasting coloured rectangles. The speckled background is worked using offcuts of woven tweed dress fabric. The design is outlined in a black border, framed in bright red.
LIZ KITCHING

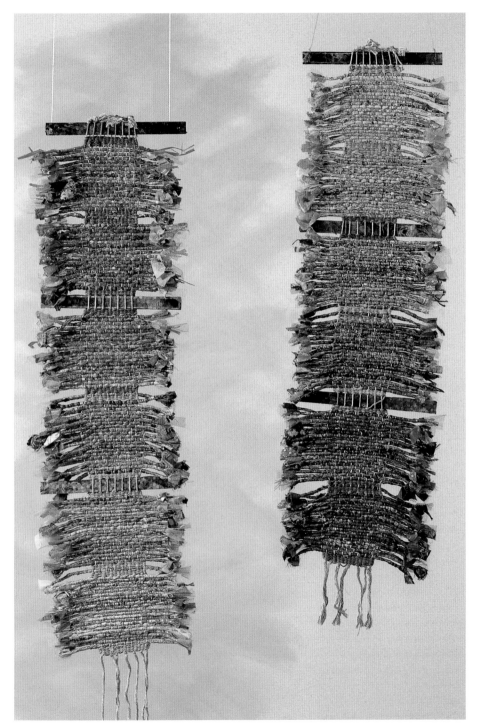

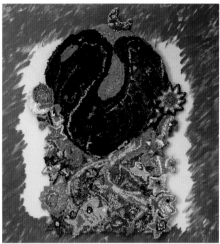

*Left:* PINKISH AND
BLUEISH
86.5 x 23 cm (34 x 9 in)
This pair of wallhangings
explores the colour
spectrums of pink and
blue. Each uses lengths of
fabric wrapped with
coloured rayon threads.
The strips are woven in an
order which enhances the
colour movement.
ANGELA HARRISON

*Above:* BLACK SWAN
183 x 122 cm (72 x 48 in)
This shaped wallpiece was
made during an artist's
residency at the Black
Swan Guild in Frome,
Somerset, where the piece
is now on permanent
display. The work was a
collaboration, created and
hooked by students from
the local college, members
of a textile group and
people with visual
impairment. The shape was
hooked on a large frame,
and smaller shapes such as
the fish, moons and stars
were made separately on
small embroidery hoops.
JULIEANN WORRALL HOOD

# MATERIALS

THE VERY ESSENCE OF RAGWORK IS THAT THE MATERIALS ARE RECYCLED, AND THEREFORE VERY INEXPENSIVE. EVEN THE MOST UNLIKELY FABRICS, SUCH AS CRIMPLENE OR UNFASHIONABLE PRINTS, ARE TRANSFORMED WHEN CUT INTO STRIPS AND MIXED WITH OTHER COLOURS AND TEXTURES. MODERN RAG RUG MAKERS EVEN USE DISCARDED PLASTIC CARRIER BAGS, CRISPS AND SWEETS PACKETS. THE OTHER INEXPENSIVE MATERIAL WIDELY USED IN RAGWORK IS HESSIAN.

**Cotton fabrics**, particularly old printed shirts and dresses or remnants, are ideal for ragwork and particularly suitable for plaiting, crochet and knitting.

**Jersey fabrics** Cotton T-shirts are lovely to work with, fray very little and are good for cut or loop pile surfaces.

**Fabric strips** A wide variety of fabric can be recycled, including old clothing, curtains and bedclothes. Cut off any fastenings and seams.

**Plastic strips** are a modern option to use with or instead of fabric. Plastic carrier bags slip easily through the hessian and create unusual textures.

**Foil strips** Add sparkle with foil-backed crisps packets and gift wrap.

**Black felt** is used as a smart backing cloth to finish jewellery, mirror frames and tablemats. Cut offcuts into strips and use in another project.

**Calico** is a cheap, lightweight cotton very suitable for internal covers for cushion pads. It can be used as a backing cloth.

**Hessian** Originally old sacking cloth was used to hook or prod through. Hessian, made from jute, has a pliable, woven construction and the warp and weft threads open and close easily. It is available in different weights – 250 g (10 oz) is perfect for ragwork.

**Tapestry canvas** has a more rigid construction and can therefore be worked without a frame. For a rug, choose a weave of three holes to 2.5 cm (1 in).

**Carpet webbing tape** is a heavy-duty woven calico tape, used to cover the edges of rugs. It comes in various widths.

**Carpet binding tape** is also used to bind edges and seams on the back of rugs.

**Thin wire** is useful in sculpted pieces. It is often used in the wrapping technique.

**Latex carpet adhesive** is used in backing finished pieces of ragwork. Use in a well-ventilated area and avoid contact with clothing.

**Clear-drying impact adhesive** is used in small amounts to stick backing cloth such as felt to smaller pieces of work.

**Superglue** is a very strong, quick-drying adhesive that is used to secure jewellery findings, such as ring fittings etc.

**Brooch clip fastenings** are available in metal in several designs. The two pictured are suitable for ragwork jewellery. The brooch bar-style fastening is sewn to the back of work, while the round-shaped fastening is best stuck on.

**Hair clip fastenings** are available in several sizes. Measure the finished hairslide shape to determine the length of the bar needed.

**Ring fittings** Made in metal, these are available in silver and gold finishes. Adjustable styles are best.

**Drinks can ring pulls** make ideal hangers for picture and mirror frames.

**Elastic hair bands** These are available in a variety of colours so you can coordinate hair accessories.

**Black sewing thread** is used to tack down edges and to slip stitch black felt backing cloth into position.

**Invisible thread** is very strong. It is used to hem finish any colour.

**Coloured sewing threads** For hard-wearing projects, use double-thickness cotton or a polyester mix sewing thread.

**Coloured viscose/rayon embroidery threads** come in a selection of bright, acidic colours. Use to bind strips of fabric in wrapping.

**Coloured cotton embroidery thread** is thicker than general sewing thread and suitable for hand-sewn decorative finishes.

1 Cotton fabrics
2 Jersey fabrics
3 Fabric strips
4 Plastic strips
5 Foil strips
6 Black felt
7 Calico
8 Hessian
9 Tapestry canvas
10 Carpet webbing tape
11 Binding tape
12 Thin wire
13 Latex carpet adhesive
14 Clear-drying impact adhesive
15 Superglue
16 Brooch clip fastening
17 Hair clip fastening
18 Ring fitting
19 Drinks can ring pulls
20 Elastic hair bands
21 Black sewing thread
22 Invisible thread
23 Coloured viscose/rayon embroidery threads
24 Coloured cotton embroidery thread

# EQUIPMENT

RAGWORK REQUIRES VERY FEW SPECIALIST TOOLS. THE EQUIPMENT NEEDED DEPENDS ON WHICH RAGWORK TECHNIQUES YOU ARE USING. PLAITING AND WRAPPING NEED LEAST EQUIPMENT OF ALL — LITTLE MORE THAN A NEEDLE AND THREAD. KNITTING AND CROCHET ARE DONE WITH ORDINARY NEEDLES. FOR HOOKING OR PRODDING, YOU NEED A FRAME OF SOME KIND. SMALL PROJECTS CAN BE WORKED IN AN EMBROIDERY HOOP.

**Masking tape** is used to stick down a tracing, prevent the raw edges of hessian fraying, or to tape the rough edges of tapestry canvas, to avoid skin irritation.

**Tape measure** This is an essential item and more flexible than a ruler.

**Dressmaker's pins** are handy to hold fabric in place before stitching.

**Safety pin** This is used in the plaiting technique.

**Sewing needles** are constantly used for finishing, especially when attaching the backing cloth. Also important in plaiting.

**Crochet hook (10 mm size)** is needed for the crochet technique and it can also be used in the hooking technique.

**Knitting needles (10 mm size)** are used for the Knitted Patchwork Rug.

**Drawing paper** It is always a good idea to draw the design first.

**White card** is used for making templates.

**Cutting mat** A plastic self-healing cutting mat prevents marking your table.

**Tracing paper** is used to sketch and transfer the design.

**String** is used in setting up a frame. Using a large-eyed needle, stitch the string through the hessian and around the frame edge to get the hessian taut.

**Craft knife** Use as an alternative to scissors for cutting out templates.

**Scissors** are essential in all ragwork projects. You need two pairs: a sharp pair for cutting fabric and a pair for cutting paper, foil and plastic, as these materials will blunt the blades.

**Marker pen** A large, black, indelible marker pen works best for marking out the design on the hessian.

**Transfer pencil** This is used to transfer the design on to the hessian. Draw over the reverse of the artwork, then iron on.

**Prodder** This is a blunt-ended wooden tool used in making a prodded, or "clippy", mat. An alternative is a large, smooth-ended wooden peg.

**Hook** This has a hand-turned yew handle with a tapering brass sharp-ended hook. It is pushed through the hessian up to the wooden handle, leaving a large hole.

**Metre rule** Use this to mark out the outline of a large rug on to hessian.

**Ruler** Use this to measure straight edges for small-scale design work.

**Large adjustable frame and pegs** The traditional wooden mat-making frame is adjustable, with two pieces of wood for the length, two (with drilled holes in which to position the pegs) for the sides, and four turned wooden pegs, one for each corner. The length can be wrapped round the frame so that you can continue working on the next area, approximately 56 cm (22 in) deep. Hessian is stapled or strung on to the frame and the pegs are then positioned one at each corner, keeping the hessian very taut. Use this for larger rugs and wall hangings.

**Embroidery hoops** are used to stretch hessian for making smaller items.

**Artist's stretchers** make a good portable frame and are available in pairs in many different lengths. Always use a frame larger than the finished piece of work.

**Pliers** are used to cut wire, particularly in the wrapping technique.

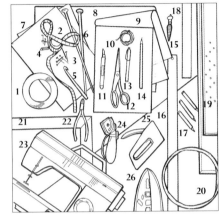

1 Masking tape
2 Tape measure
3 Dressmaker's pins
4 Safety pin
5 Crochet hook (10 mm size)
6 Knitting needles (10 mm size)
7 Drawing paper
8 Cutting mat
9 Tracing paper
10 String
11 Craft knife
12 Scissors
13 Marker pen
14 Transfer pencil
15 Prodder
16 Hook
17 Metre rule
18 Ruler
19 Large adjustable frame and pegs
20 Embroidery hoop
21 Artist's stretchers
22 Pliers
23 Sewing machine
24 Rotary cutter
25 Staple gun
26 Iron

**Sewing machine** This is not an essential item, but very helpful for stitching appliqué and hems.

**Rotary cutter** This is useful for quickly cutting layers of fabric into strips.

**Staple gun** This can be used to attach the hessian to the frame quickly.

**Iron** Hessian is usually supplied either rolled or folded, so you may need to iron out any creases.

# BASIC TECHNIQUES

SIX RAGWORK TECHNIQUES ARE USED IN THIS BOOK — HOOKING, PRODDING, PLAITING, CROCHET, KNITTING AND WRAPPING. EACH TECHNIQUE HAS ITS OWN CHARACTERISTICS AND EACH IS SUITABLE FOR DIFFERENT ITEMS, AS ILLUS-TRATED IN THE PROJECTS. THIS CHAPTER GIVES STEP-BY-STEP INSTRUCTIONS FOR EACH OF THE SIX BASIC TECHNIQUES, SO IT IS IMPORTANT TO READ THIS SECTION BEFORE BEGINNING THE PROJECTS.

## HOOKING

This is the most common technique used in ragwork, and also the most versatile. It lends itself to recycling and can revitalize many redundant materials, including plastics and foil as well as a huge range of fabrics, both natural and synthetic.

Strips of these materials are worked, or hooked, through a hessian backing cloth. They can be left as a loop pile surface, or sheared with scissors to create a cut pile surface. An effective use of hooking is to combine cut and loop pile within one piece. This gives a sculpted, three-dimensional appearance, as you can see in the Queen of Hearts and Mythological Beast projects.

1 Place one hand underneath the frame, and loop a strip of fabric between your thumb and forefinger. With your other hand above the frame, push the hook through the hessian. Feed the fabric loop on to the hook. (The picture shows what is happening from the underside of the frame.)

2 Pull the hook back up through the hessian, bringing the end of the strip of fabric through to the top.

3 Leave 1–2 warp threads of hessian to keep the loops close together. Push the hook back through the hessian and feed the fabric loop on to the hook, as before. Pull the hook back up through the hessian to make a loop, approximately 1 cm (½ in) high. Continue. Bring the ends of fabric through to the top, and trim to the same height as the loops.

4 To create a cut pile surface, repeat steps 1–3 but hook the loops to a height of approximately 2 cm (¾ in). Shear across the top of the loops with a large pair of scissors.

### SAMPLE SWATCHES OF HOOKED MATERIALS

The most unlikely fabrics and materials can be incorporated within your work, and recycling is a natural, traditional approach to exploring the technique of hooking.

### Sea Green Knitted Cotton Jersey T-shirt Fabric

Works well for both cut and loop pile surfaces. Results in a highly durable surface, suitable for rugs.
**Loop pile:** colour appears lighter than when cut.
**Cut pile:** darker pile, spiral texture.

### Red Foil Crisps Packets

Loop pile gives the most interesting results. Good for jewellery and other fashion accessories.
**Loop pile:** highlights a shiny surface.
**Cut pile:** appears dull and darker in tone.

*Left: All the fabrics and materials used in these swatches have been recycled. Reading from left to right, each group of three shows (a) the original material or fabric, (b) loop pile and (c) cut pile.*

**Key:**

1 Sea green knitted cotton jersey T-shirt fabric
2 Red foil crisps packets
3 Tan-coloured nylon tights
4 Petrol blue knitted woollen dress fabric
5 Rust-coloured satin coat lining fabric
6 Denim jeans
7 Mint green patterned crimplene dress fabric
8 Green plastic carrier bag
9 Lemon yellow acrylic/ wool blanket
10 Red tartan kilt fabric

**Denim Jeans**

Denim can be used by itself to great effect, combining washed and faded denim with darker indigo shades. Very hard-wearing, hooked denim floor rugs have a long lifespan.

**Loop pile:** extremely durable, hard on the hands to work with.

**Cut pile:** more subtle effect. To help your hands, cut small areas from time to time as you hook.

**Mint Green Patterned Crimplene Dress Fabric**

Not known for its beauty in its former life but very effective here. Numerous uses in interior and fashion projects.

**Loop pile:** shows the texture and surface pattern well.

**Cut pile:** easy to cut, with a spiral surface texture.

**Green Plastic Carrier Bag**

Slips through the hessian with the greatest of ease! Waterproof – suitable for bathmats, jewellery, wall pieces.

**Loop pile:** bead-like looped surface.

**Cut pile:** jagged surface texture, darker colour.

**Lemon Yellow Acrylic/Wool Blanket**

Cut thicker, heavier weight fabric into thinner strips. Excellent wearing properties, this is most suitable for floor rugs.

**Loop pile:** can appear quite bulky.

**Cut pile:** felt-like surface, good as a background filler, quick to work.

**Red Tartan Kilt Fabric**

Woven and printed fabrics help to break up areas of flat colour. Little difference between the look of the loop and cut surfaces. Good for decoration.

**Loop pile:** frays slightly, more durable than when cut.

**Cut pile:** tends to fray.

**Tan-coloured Nylon Tights**

Works with both surfaces, quite diverse results. Suitable for most projects. Try other colours.

**Loop pile:** small, rounded looped surface; easy to hook.

**Cut pile:** good for blending areas of colour together.

**Petrol Blue Knitted Woollen Dress Fabric**

This fabric felts when machine-washed on a high temperature setting. Versatile, good for use in any project.

**Loop pile:** soft texture.

**Cut pile:** surface colour appears darker when cut.

**Rust-coloured Satin Coat Lining Fabric**

Look beyond a coat's exterior – linings are available in many colours. Most suitable for hats, bags and wallhangings.

**Loop pile:** enhances colour, can fray slightly, and particularly good mixed with other materials.

**Cut pile:** darker surface colour, tends to fray considerably.

## PRODDING

The prodding technique is also known as proggie, peggy, tabbie, poked and brodded, to name but a few of the regional variations. Traditionally wool clippings from old, worn clothing and blankets were used to make "clippy" mats.

This technique is worked from the reverse side of the backing. Prodding creates a deep, shaggy surface and works well for soft, thick textured rugs or wallhangings. Designs tend to have an impressionistic look, as the details are blurred due to the surface pile.

**1** Prepare the fabrics by cutting them into clippings 7 x 1½ cm (2¾ x ¾ in). Working on the underside of the frame, make a hole with the tapered end of the prodder. Take a clipping and prod it halfway through the hessian, using the prodder. Use your other hand on the other side to catch and pull the fabric down to approximately half its length.

**2** Make another hole with the prodder a bit less than 1 cm (½ in) away, or 4–5 warp threads of hessian.

**3** Prod the other end of the clipping through this hole. Using your hand underneath, tug both ends of the clipping until they are of even length. Continue by prodding the next clipping through the same hole as the end of the first clipping.

## PLAITING

Plaiting is strongly associated with American folk art. Three strips of fabric are first plaited together. The plaits are then joined by machine or hand stitched. They can be wound into circular shapes or worked into square or rectangular rugs.

**1** Plaiting is much easier if you first fasten the ends of the fabric strips together with a safety pin, and hook this over a cuphook screwed into the wall. Start the plaiting near the safety pin. Bring the righthand strip over the middle strip, then bring the lefthand strip over the new middle strip. Continue plaiting, turning the raw edges under as much as possible, until you are left with about 20 cm (8 in) unplaited. Secure the end with a pin.

**2** Remove the safety pin and taper the beginning of the plait, trimming as necessary. Stitch neatly to conceal the raw edges when joining the plaits.

## CROCHET

In recent years, experimental crochet work has moved away from the tradition of using wool. Using fabric strips creates beautifully subtle changes within colour tones, and the technique works well in three-dimensional projects, such as the Crochet Duffel Bag.

Crochet is also useful for joining knitted pieces together.

### Abbreviations

ch: chain; dc: double crochet; lp: loop; sc: single crochet; st: stitch; sl st: slip stitch; tr: treble; yoh: yarn over hook

### MAKING FOUNDATION CHAIN

Chain stitch is the foundation stitch on to which further stitches are worked. Make a slip loop to form first stitch. Yoh, draw through lp. Repeat until ch reaches desired length.

## SLIP STITCH

This is used for joining pieces.
Sl st, skip 1 ch, insert hook under top lp of next ch. Yoh, draw through ch and lp on hook (1 sl st formed). Repeat to end of ch. Turn, make 1 ch and continue, working next sl st under both lps of 2nd st from hook. Work last sl st of row into last ch.

## DOUBLE CROCHET

This is used to edge knitting.
Skip 1 ch, insert hook under top lp of next ch. Yoh, draw through ch only. Yoh and draw through both lps on hook (1 dc formed). Repeat to end of ch. Work last dc of row into last ch. Turn, make 1 ch and continue, working the next dc under both lps of 2nd st from hook.

## TREBLE

Very durable, this is ideal for the bases of various bags.
Skip 3 ch, yoh, insert hook under top lp of next ch, yoh and draw through ch only (3 lps on hook). Yoh, draw through next 2 lps on hook (2 lps on hook). Yoh, draw through 2 remaining lps on hook (1 tr formed). Repeat to end of ch. Turn, make 3 ch and continue, working next tr under both lps of 2nd st from hook. Work last tr of row into the last ch of previous row.

# KNITTING

Knitting with fabric strips is an interesting and fun alternative to using wool. Patterned cotton fabrics work particularly well – as the number of stitches grows on the needles, both the top and underside of the fabrics are exposed, revealing softer tones within the colour variations. For a patchwork effect, knit squares of different fabric strips and join together with crochet.

## CASTING ON

Make a slip loop on the left needle to form the first stitch. Insert the right needle through the loop. Wrap the yarn forward, under and over the right needle. Draw the new loop through the slip loop and pass it on to the left needle. Repeat to create as many stitches as you need.

## PLAIN KNIT OR GARTER STITCH

Plain knit, or garter, stitch is the simplest of all knitting stitches. Every stitch of every row is knitted. Hold the working needle in your right hand like a pencil.
    Insert the right needle through the first loop on the left needle. Wrap the yarn forward, under and over the right needle. Draw the stitch forward and under and slip it off the left needle on to the right. Repeat to the end of the row, then turn the work and knit the next row.

## CASTING OFF

Knit the first two stitches as usual. Insert the left needle under the first stitch made, from left to right. Lift the stitch up and over the second stitch and over the point of the needle. Knit the next stitch from the left needle and repeat the process to the end of the row. Cut the end of the yarn and draw it through the final stitch to finish off.

## WRAPPING

This technique uses very little material. Strips of fabrics are bound together with coloured embroidery threads to create wallhangings. Wire can be added to create beautiful, sculptural jewellery.

1 Select three different fabrics, and cut into strips 1 cm (½ in) wide. Choose a coloured embroidery thread to enhance the fabrics' colours. Pinch the strips tightly together in one hand. Working from the right, with the other hand start to bind the thread closely around the fabric strips.

2 Continue binding with the thread until you wish to change the fabric. Add a loop of thicker yarn, with the loop facing the end you have been working from. Continue to wrap the thread around this.

3 Thread the remaining embroidery thread through the loop. Pull the two ends of the thicker looped yarn towards the left until the thread is fastened off.

## BACKING

Traditionally rag rugs were rarely finished with a backing fabric, but it does make floor rugs more durable, as well as looking neat. If you are making a fashion accessory or a piece of jewellery, backing it with a softer fabric such as felt will prevent the hessian used in the ragwork from fraying and perhaps irritating the skin.

### HESSIAN

Hessian is a cheap backing fabric for rugs, and easy to apply. Use carpet webbing tape to cover the raw edges if wished.

1 Apply a thin layer of latex adhesive over the back of the work, and leave to dry for 3–5 minutes. Cut a piece of hessian slightly larger than the work, to allow for a border. Stick down.

2 Apply a thin layer of latex adhesive to the border and leave to dry for 3–5 minutes. Fold over the border and stick down firmly. Trim any excess hessian with scissors to neaten the backing.

### FELT

Use felt to back fashion and interior accessories, such as brooches, earrings, mirror frames and tablemats.

Coloured felt can be chosen to coordinate with the colours used in the design. Alternatively, black felt looks good as a backing for any colour, and does not discolour or pick up dirt.

1 Using the finished ragwork as a template, cut out a slightly larger piece of felt. Pin round the edge to attach it in position on the back of the work. Take a needle and matching thread, and slip stitch round the edge, tucking under the excess fabric as you sew.

## OTHER FINISHING METHODS

As well as backing with fabric, there are two other recommended ways to finish pieces of ragwork neatly and securely.

### STITCHING

One option for finishing ragwork is to stitch around the border area to secure the excess backing cloth. This is most suitable for pieces with straight edges.

1 Cut round the finished piece, leaving a border of at least 2 cm (¾ in). Fold the excess hessian to the back and pin, turning under the raw edges.

2 Take a needle and double cotton thread, and slip stitch the hessian border neatly to the back of the work.

### LATEX ADHESIVE

This is rubberized carpet adhesive which contains a strong bonding agent. There are many advantages in using latex, particularly to finish irregularly shaped work, such as shaped mirror frames, circular rugs and jewellery.

Always use latex in a well-ventilated area. Latex will rub off your hands but not off your clothes, so an apron or protective clothing is advisable.

1 Cut round the finished piece of the work, leaving a border of at least 2 cm (¾ in). Using a piece of stiff card or suitable applicator, spread a thin layer of latex over the back of the work. Leave to dry for 3–5 minutes.

2 Fold in the edges of the ragwork. If you are working on a circular, curved or irregularly shaped piece, snip the border at intervals first.

3 Cut off any excess hessian and stick the edges down firmly. The underside of your work should be as flat as possible.

## A NOTE ABOUT FRAMES

Ragwork makers usually keep a variety of frames. Most will have an adjustable frame as described in the Equipment section, which is invaluable for large rugs and useful in that the size can be adjusted to suit a particular piece of work. Hessian can be attached to these types of frame by stapling or stringing. Some makes have strips of binding tape attached to two sides on to which the hessian can be stretched and sewn.

Artist's stretchers can be purchased in pairs in different lengths to make square or rectangular frames to a specific size. Hessian can be attached to these frames by stapling or stringing, or carpet webbing tape can be sewn to two sides of the hessian and then stapled to the frame.

Beginners will not want to invest in a wide range of frames to begin with. Therefore, it is important to note that the amounts of hessian specified in the individual projects relate to the size of the finished work, plus a border allowance for finishing and attaching the hessian to a frame a little larger than the finished piece. You can use a larger frame, but make sure you purchase sufficient hessian to cover it.

# CRISPY JEWELLERY

EVEN CRISPS PACKETS CAN BE RECYCLED IN RAGWORK! THE SHINY FOIL IS PERFECT FOR MODERN JEWELLERY, AND IT CAN BE CUT INTO STRIPS AND HOOKED TO MAKE A LOOP PILE SURFACE JUST LIKE FABRIC OR YARN. HERE THE FOIL IN THE MIDDLE OF THE HEART-SHAPED BROOCH CONTRASTS BEAUTIFULLY WITH THE DARK FABRIC BORDER. THE MATCHING RING IS MADE FOLLOWING THE SAME INSTRUCTIONS. THE CARD TEMPLATES USED FOR BOTH SHAPES ARE VERY EASY TO MAKE. YOU COULD ALSO DESIGN OTHER SIMPLE BROOCH SHAPES, SUCH AS A STAR, A CRESCENT MOON OR A FLOWER.

1 Make a card template for the brooch. Draw a heart shape approximately 8 cm (3 in) across. Place the template on the hessian and draw round it, using a marker pen. Put the hessian into the embroidery hoop.

3 Cut the crisps packets into strips 1 cm (½ in) wide. Fill in the centre of the heart shape with loops of the same height as the fabric loops. Bring all the ends through to the top of the work, and trim any excess lengths.

5 Using scissors, snip the border in towards the design at regular intervals. Turn in the edges and press down firmly. Apply small dabs of clear adhesive to the back of the work, then cover with the black felt. Slip stitch around the edge.

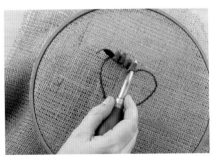

2 Cut the dark green fabric into strips 1 cm (½ in) wide. Begin hooking, following the outline of the heart shape. Make close loops, approximately 1 cm (½ in) high.

4 Remove the hessian from the hoop and cut around the shape, allowing a border of 2.5 cm (1 in). Apply a thin layer of latex adhesive to the back and the border. Leave to dry for 3–5 minutes.

6 Place the clip fastening on the back of the brooch. Stitch, using double thread. To make the ring, use a 2.5 cm (1 in) diameter circle for the template. Attach the ring fitting with superglue.

MATERIALS AND EQUIPMENT YOU WILL NEED

CARD • SCISSORS • HESSIAN, 30 x 30 CM (12 x 12 IN) • MARKER PEN • EMBROIDERY HOOP • DARK FABRIC • HOOK • FOIL CRISPS PACKETS • LATEX CARPET ADHESIVE AND APPLICATOR • CLEAR-DRYING IMPACT ADHESIVE • BLACK FELT, 12 x 12 CM (5 x 5 IN) • NEEDLE AND MATCHING THREAD • BROOCH CLIP FASTENING • RING FITTING • SUPERGLUE

# HANDBAG MIRROR FRAME

MAKE THIS SMALL-SCALE RAGWORK PROJECT AS AN ORIGINAL PRESENT FOR A FRIEND OR RELATIVE. THIS BRIGHT PINK JERSEY FABRIC CONTRASTS STRONGLY WITH THE SHINY YELLOW FOIL, BUT YOU CAN USE ANY COMBINATION OF TWO COLOURS. SMALL PROJECTS LIKE THIS ARE VERY QUICK AND SATISFYING TO MAKE. THEY DEMONSTRATE HOW WHAT WAS TRADITIONALLY A RUG TECHNIQUE CAN BE UPDATED AND USED FOR MANY OTHER DESIGNS, SMALL OR LARGE.

1 Make a card template measuring 9 x 8 cm (3½ x 3 in), with a frame depth of 2.5 cm (1 in). Place in the centre of the hessian and draw round both the outer and inner edges, using a marker pen.

3 Work the pink fabric round the inner rectangle. Hook a second rectangle, using the yellow foil. Complete the frame with a final row in pink fabric.

5 Cut a cross into the corners of the inner rectangle. Turn under the edges and press down firmly. Trim any excess hessian. Apply small dabs of clear adhesive on the back, then cover with one of the pieces of felt. Slip stitch together. Carefully cut out the centre.

2 Put the hessian into the embroidery hoop. Cut both the fabric and the foil packets into strips 1 cm (½ in) wide. Start hooking the frame with the pink fabric, beginning just beyond and outside one edge of the inner rectangle.

4 Remove the hessian from the embroidery hoop, and place face down on a flat surface. Cut round the outer shape, allowing an extra border of 2.5 cm (1 in). Apply a thin layer of latex adhesive over the back, including the central area and the border. Leave to dry for 3–5 minutes.

6 Use the other piece of felt to make a pocket. Pin it to the back of the mirror frame, then blanket-stitch round three sides. Leave the fourth side open to slide in the mirror.

## MATERIALS AND EQUIPMENT YOU WILL NEED

CARD • RULER • SCISSORS • HESSIAN, 25 x 25 CM (10 x 10 IN) • MARKER PEN • EMBROIDERY HOOP • PINK COTTON JERSEY FABRIC • HOOK • YELLOW FOIL CRISPS OR SWEETS PACKETS • LATEX CARPET ADHESIVE AND APPLICATOR • CLEAR-DRYING IMPACT ADHESIVE • TWO PIECES OF BLACK FELT, EACH 9 x 8 CM (3½ x 3 IN) • NEEDLE AND MATCHING THREAD • DRESSMAKER'S PINS • MIRROR, 8 x 7 CM (3 x 2¾ IN)

# STRIPED HALL RUNNER

THIS BOLD DESIGN OF STARS AND STRIPES WAS INSPIRED BY 1950s TEXTILES. THE BLACK AT EITHER END AND BETWEEN THE STRIPES CONTRASTS WITH THE OTHER COLOURS, MAKING THEM SEEM EVEN BRIGHTER. BEFORE BEGINNING THIS PROJECT, YOU NEED TO SORT THE FABRICS INTO SEPARATE COLOUR GROUPS. USE A MIXTURE OF FABRICS, BLENDING WOOL AND LYCRA WITH COTTON AND CRIMPLENE TO CREATE A CUT PILE SURFACE WHICH IS VERY HARDWEARING FOR A FLOOR RUG. ALTERNATIVELY, YOU COULD ADAPT THE DESIGN TO MAKE A SMALLER RUNNER TO SIT ON TOP OF A PINE CHEST.

1 Using a marker pen, draw a rectangle measuring 100 x 46 cm (40 x 18½ in) on the larger piece of hessian. Allow an extra border of at least 13 cm (5 in) all round. Working within the rectangle, draw a panel at each end measuring 11.5 cm (4½ in) deep. Draw four star motifs evenly spaced across each panel, as shown. Sort the fabrics into groups of each colour. Cut into strips 1 cm (½ in) wide.

2 Using a staple gun, attach the hessian to the frame. Hook the star motifs, as shown, working the loops close together. Shear across the top of the loops with scissors to create a cut pile surface.

4 When the panel at this end is complete, you can start the striped part of the runner. Hook the first horizontal stripe right across the width.  ▶

3 Fill in the panel background with black fabric. Bring the ends of the fabric strips through to the top of the work, and trim off any excess.

## MATERIALS AND EQUIPMENT YOU WILL NEED
MARKER PEN • RULER • TWO PIECES OF HESSIAN, AT LEAST 126 x 72 CM (50 x 28½ IN) AND 100 x 46 CM (40 x 18½ IN) • STAPLE GUN • WOODEN FRAME • ASSORTED FABRICS, IN BLACK, PINK, MINT GREEN, NAVY, RED, YELLOW AND BLUE • HOOK • SCISSORS • LATEX CARPET ADHESIVE AND APPLICATOR • CARPET WEBBING TAPE, 3.5 M (3½ YD)

**5** The colour sequence repeats every eighth row. To work the black and red stripes hook two rows, for the other stripes hook one row. Continue hooking up to the other panel. Fill in the panel design as before.

**6** Remove the runner from the frame, and lay face down. Cut round the design, allowing a border of at least 5 cm (2 in).

**7** Apply a thin layer of latex adhesive to the back of the runner. Leave to dry for 3–5 minutes.

**8** Take the second piece of hessian and place this over the back of the runner. Press and smooth down.

**9** Spread a thin layer of latex adhesive on the border of the runner. Leave to dry for 2 minutes. Turn over the border, folding in the corners. Cut off any excess hessian to leave a flat surface.

**10** Cut the carpet webbing tape to give two lengths measuring 100 cm (40 in) and two measuring 46 cm (18 in). Smear a thin layer of latex adhesive on one side of the tape, and stick over the raw edges of the hessian backing cloth. Leave the runner to dry overnight.

# RECTANGULAR FLOWER RUG

BRING SUMMER INDOORS WITH THIS CHARMING LITTLE FLOWER FRAMED IN A TRELLIS BORDER. THE DIAMONDS OF THE TRELLIS AND THE FLOWER ARE OUTLINED FIRST IN A DARK COLOUR, WHICH GIVES EMPHASIS TO THE DESIGN AND CONTRASTS WITH THE SUBTLE, RANDOM COLOURS AND TEXTURES USED TO FILL IN THE REST OF THE RUG. A MIXTURE OF FABRICS WAS USED HERE, INCLUDING TWEED OFFCUTS AND COTTON JERSEY. CONTRAST THE BRIGHT COLOURS YOU CHOOSE FOR THE CENTRAL FLOWER PANEL WITH THE SOFTER COLOURS OF THE TRELLIS BORDER.

1 Using a marker pen, draw a rectangle measuring 80 x 60 cm (32 x 24 in) on the larger piece of hessian. Allow an extra border of 8 cm (3 in) all round. Draw the flower design in the centre, then use a ruler to mark out the trellis border.

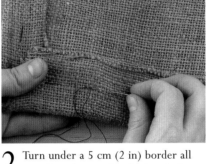

2 Turn under a 5 cm (2 in) border all round, and pin and tack. Attach the hessian to the frame by stringing (see Chirpy Chair Pad) or by sewing the border to the bonding tape attached to an adjustable frame.

4 Fill in the diamonds, working in rows and using a variety of rich colours. ▶

3 Hook the trellis shapes, using a dark coloured fabric. Make the loops approximately 5 mm (¼ in) high.

MATERIALS AND EQUIPMENT YOU WILL NEED

TWO PIECES OF HESSIAN, AT LEAST 96 x 76 CM (38 x 30 IN) AND 90 x 70 CM (36 x 28 IN) • MARKER PEN • RULER • DRESSMAKER'S PINS • NEEDLE AND STRONG THREAD • WOODEN FRAME • STRING • LARGE-EYED NEEDLE • HOOK • ASSORTED FABRICS, INCLUDING TWEED AND COTTON JERSEY • CARPET BINDING TAPE, 3.5 M (3½ YD)

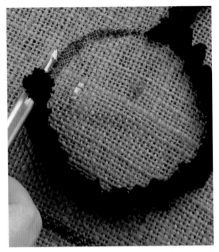

5 Hook the central flower motif, using a dark colour. Start by working the stalk, then move up towards the outline of the flower head.

6 Fill in the centre of the flower head, using a bright colour.

7 Continue hooking until all areas of the design are filled.

8 Remove the rug from the frame. Take the second piece of hessian, turn under the excess fabric and pin to the back of the rug, with the raw edges inside. Using double thread, tack round the edge.

9 Cut the carpet binding tape into four strips, measuring the same length as the four sides of the rug. Roll the ends of the tape and stitch to prevent fraying.

10 Pin the tape in position to cover the hessian border round the rug. Slip stitch to the front and back.

# GEOMETRIC HAIRBAND

THE LONG, RECTANGULAR SHAPE OF THIS HAIRBAND LENDS ITSELF TO A BOLD REPEAT PATTERN OF SQUARES OR TRIANGLES. TWO DIFFERENT BUT EQUALLY SIMPLE DESIGNS HAVE BEEN SHOWN HERE FOR INSPIRATION. ALTERNATIVELY, YOU COULD WORK OUT YOUR OWN DESIGN AND COLOUR SCHEME ON GRAPH PAPER — TRY HOOKING SMALL FLOWERS OR HEART SHAPES FOR A COMPLETELY DIFFERENT LOOK. NYLON FABRICS HAVE BEEN USED IN THIS PROJECT, BUT YOU COULD USE COTTONS OR A MIXTURE OF FABRICS. THE HAIRBAND IS FASTENED VERY SIMPLY WITH MATCHING RIBBON TIES.

1 Make a rectangular card template measuring 32 x 4 cm (12½ x 1½ in). Place in the centre of the hessian and draw round it, using a marker pen. Use a staple gun to attach the hessian to the frame.

3 Fill in the shapes, using contrasting fabrics alternately. Shear across the tops of the loops periodically as the work progresses.

5 Turn in the border and press down firmly. Apply small dabs of clear adhesive on the back, then cover with the black felt. Slip stitch the felt in place, turning under any excess fabric.

2 Cut the fabrics into strips 1 cm (½ in) wide. Begin by hooking the outline of your chosen design, working in close loops. Shear across the tops of the loops to create a cut pile surface.

4 When the design is completed, remove the hessian from the frame. Cut round the hooked rectangle, allowing an extra border of at least 2.5 cm (1 in). Apply a thin layer of latex adhesive over the back, including the border. Leave to dry for 3–5 minutes.

6 Pin the ribbon along the centre back of the hairband, leaving equal lengths at each end to make the ties. Stitch the ribbon in place.

MATERIALS AND EQUIPMENT YOU WILL NEED

CARD • RULER • HESSIAN, 61 x 30 CM (24 x 12 IN) • MARKER PEN • STAPLE GUN • WOODEN FRAME •
NYLON FABRICS, IN ASSORTED COLOURS • HOOK • SCISSORS • LATEX CARPET ADHESIVE AND APPLICATOR •
CLEAR-DRYING IMPACT ADHESIVE • BLACK FELT, 33 x 5 CM (13 x 2 IN) • NEEDLE AND MATCHING THREAD • DRESSMAKER'S PINS •
RIBBON, 1 M (1 YD)

# STARRY TABLEMAT

MAKE MATS FOR YOUR TABLE AS WELL AS YOUR FLOOR! THIS IS AN IDEAL SMALL PROJECT TO EXPERIMENT WITH. THE DESIGN IS VERY SIMPLE, AS IS THE COLOUR SCHEME. USE A VARIETY OF TONES OF BLUE AND RED TO GIVE EXTRA INTEREST. THE CUT PILE SURFACE AND FELT BACKING ARE VERY PRACTICAL, AND WILL PROTECT YOUR TABLETOP AS WELL AS LOOKING GOOD. YOU CAN ALSO MAKE A MATCHING COASTER, REVERSING THE COLOUR SCHEME TO HOOK A RED STAR ON A BLUE BACKGROUND. EXPERIMENT WITH OTHER SIMPLE MOTIFS AND COLOURS, OR CREATE A DESIGN FOR A RECTANGULAR TABLEMAT.

1 Draw a 30 cm (12 in) diameter circle on the card, and cut out. Position the circle on the hessian, and draw round it with a marker pen. Measure in 4 cm (1½ in) and draw an inner circle, then draw a third circle in between the other two.

3 Outline the star in navy fabrics, then begin working the red background. When you have completed a small area, shear across the top of the loops to create a cut pile surface.

5 Apply a thin layer of latex adhesive to the back of the tablemat and the border. Leave to dry for 3–5 minutes. Snip into the border at regular intervals, then turn in on to the back of the tablemat. Leave to dry for a further 30 minutes.

2 Draw an eight-pointed star in the centre. Using a staple gun, attach the hessian to the frame. Hook the star, using blue fabrics. Bring the ends of the fabric strips through to the top.

4 Work the circles in blue and navy fabrics, as shown. When the design is completed, remove the hessian from the frame. Cut round the tablemat, allowing an extra border of at least 5 cm (2 in).

6 Pin the felt to the back of the tablemat, turning the edges to make it fit. Slip stitch in position.

## MATERIALS AND EQUIPMENT YOU WILL NEED

LARGE PIECE OF CARD • SCISSORS • MARKER PEN • HESSIAN, 50 x 50 CM (20 x 20 IN) • STAPLE GUN • WOODEN FRAME • ASSORTED FABRICS, IN SHADES OF BLUE, NAVY AND RED • HOOK • LATEX CARPET ADHESIVE AND APPLICATOR • BLACK FELT, 32 CM (12½ IN) DIAMETER CIRCLE • DRESSMAKER'S PINS • NEEDLE AND MATCHING THREAD

# CROCHET DUFFEL BAG

CROCHET AND RAGWORK ARE AN IDEAL COMBINATION, USING LARGE BALLS OF CONTINUOUS FABRIC STRIPS. THE RESULT IS A STRONG, HARDWEARING BAG, WHICH IS ALSO A PERFECT SUMMER ACCESSORY FOR A DAY ON THE BEACH. COLLECT OLD STRIPED AND PATTERNED SHIRTS FROM YOUR FAMILY AND FRIENDS, OR FROM JUMBLE SALES. CHOOSE SUBTLE, TONING COLOURS FOR A FADED, SEASIDE LOOK – THE THEME IS ACCENTUATED BY THE WHITE CORD DRAWSTRING AND BRASS RINGS. THE BAG IS WORKED IN TREBLES THROUGHOUT. WORK OVER THE LOOSE ENDS OF THE PREVIOUS ROW, TO CONCEAL THEM.

**1** Cut the shirts into flat pieces discarding the collars, cuffs and yokes. Cut the fabric into strips 2 cm (¾ in) wide. To make continuous strips, cut the fabric to within 1 cm (½ in) of the edge then make another long cut parallel to the first. Clip the square corners as you work, and wind the strip into a ball. Make the base of the bag as follows, using a different colour for each round. Make the foundation loop from 6 ch and join with sl st.
**Round 1** 3 ch, 14 tr into loop, join with sl st to 3rd ch, finish off.
**Round 2** 3 ch, (1 tr into 1 tr, 2 tr into next tr) to end of round. Join with sl st to 3rd ch, finish off.
**Round 3** 3 ch, (2 tr into 2 tr, 2 tr into next tr) to end of round. Join with sl st to 3rd ch, finish off.
**Round 4** 3 ch, (2 tr into 2 tr, 2 tr into next tr) to end of round. Join with sl st to 3rd ch.

**2** Work the rest of the bag as a tube, using a different colour for each round. Make 45 ch and join to form a loop.
**Round 1** 3 ch, 1 tr into each ch to end of round. Join with sl st to 3rd ch, finish off.
**Round 2 and all subsequent rows**
3 ch, 1 tr into 1 tr to end of round. Join with sl st to 3rd ch, finish off.
Work 19 rounds altogether.

**3** With right sides together, pin the base to the lower edge of the tube, then join the two pieces together with dc. Oversew the D rings round the top edge, using double thickness thread and spacing them evenly.

**4** Thread the cord through the rings, passing both ends through the last ring. Take the ends of the cord to the base of the bag and stitch securely.

MATERIALS AND EQUIPMENT YOU WILL NEED

APPROXIMATELY FIVE OLD COTTON SHIRTS, IN STRIPED AND PATTERNED FABRICS • SCISSORS • CROCHET HOOK, 10 MM SIZE • DRESSMAKER'S PINS • NEEDLE AND MATCHING THREAD • THICK WHITE COTTON CORD, 1.5 M (1½ YD) • EIGHT BRASS D RINGS

# KNITTED PATCHWORK RUG

KNITTING WITH FABRIC IS MUCH THE SAME AS KNITTING WITH YARN, BUT ON A LARGER SCALE. THE PATCHWORK EFFECT IN THIS RUG IS ACHIEVED BY SEWING TOGETHER NARROW STRIPS OF KNITTING, WHICH ARE QUICK AND EASY TO WORK. SIMPLE CROCHET STITCHES GIVE CONTRAST AND MAKE A FIRM BORDER TO FINISH THE RUG. THE RUG MEASURES 60 x 75 CM (24 x 30 IN), BUT YOU CAN REPEAT THE DESIGN TO MAKE WHATEVER SIZE YOU WISH.

1 Cut the fabrics into continuous strips approximately 2 cm (¾ in) wide. To make continuous strips, cut the fabric to within 1 cm (½ in) of the edge of the fabric, then make another long cut parallel to the first. Clip the square corners as you work, and wind the strips into a ball.

2 Each block is made up from three knitted strips. You will need 12 strips to make the rug. Cast on ten stitches.

3 Knit 12 rows of garter stitch in the first fabric. Keep a fairly loose tension because, unlike wool, there is no "give" in the fabric strips.

4 Plan the colours to give a chequer-board effect of light and dark patches. Cut off the first fabric, leaving a loose end of 2 cm (¾ in). To join on the second fabric, fold the loose end over the first 2 cm (¾ in) of the new strip and stitch.

5 Knit 12 rows, then join in the third colour. Knit 12 rows. Cast off loosely. Neaten the ends by stitching them to the wrong side.

6 Join the strips together, using a double length of thread. With right sides together, pin and then overstitch the long edges, matching up the colour joins. Make four blocks, each of three strips. Press lightly from the back. ▶

MATERIALS AND EQUIPMENT YOU WILL NEED
COTTON PRINT FABRICS, IN ASSORTED COLOURS • SCISSORS • PAIR OF KNITTING NEEDLES, 10 MM SIZE • NEEDLE AND STRONG LINEN THREAD • DRESSMAKER'S PINS • CROCHET HOOK, 10 MM SIZE

7 Edge each block with double crochet. Starting at the top righthand corner, work 1 dc into the top of each cast-off knit stitch, then work 1 dc into the side of each knitted stitch along the lefthand edge. Work 1 dc into each bottom loop of the cast-on edge and into the side of each knitted stitch along the righthand edge.

8 Finish off and join on a second colour for round 2. Work 1 dc into 1 dc and 3 dc into 1 dc at each corner. Crochet over the loose end of fabric from the first row to conceal it.

9 Use a different colour fabric to join the first two rectangles together along the long edges. With wrong sides together, work 1 sc through the top loops of the dc on the previous rounds.

10 Using the same colour fabric, work 1 dc into each dc around the outer edge, and 3 dc into each corner stitch. Repeat these two steps to join the two remaining rectangles.

11 Join the two large rectangles together along the long edges with sc in the same way.

12 Work one more round of dc around the outside edge to finish off. Neaten the loose end of fabric by stitching it to the back of the rug.

# PAISLEY CLIPPY MAT

THE "CLIPPY" MAT IS YET ANOTHER VARIATION OF THE RAG RUG TECHNIQUE, AND VERY TRADITIONAL. INSTEAD OF STRIPS, THE FABRICS ARE CUT INTO SHORT CLIPPINGS. THE RESULT IS A THICK-PILE, SOFT-TEXTURED MAT, MADE FROM ALL-WOOLLEN FABRICS. PAISLEY MOTIFS MAKE A LOVELY, SUBTLE DESIGN, USING A PALETTE OF PASTEL SHADES WHICH COMPLEMENTS THE SOFTNESS OF THE FABRICS. WOOL RUGS AND MATS GROW OLD GRACEFULLY – THEY WEAR WELL, THEY DO NOT FLATTEN AND THEY THROW OFF THE DIRT. YOU CAN RECYCLE OLD COATS AND BLANKETS IN THIS MAT AS WELL AS DISCARDED KNITWEAR.

1 Decide on a colour scheme and collect woollen fabrics in these colours. Draw your design on tracing paper.

3 Turn under a 2.5 cm (1 in) hem all round the hessian rectangle. Pin and then stitch the hem, using running stitch.

5 To make the clippings, cut the fabrics into pieces measuring 7 x 1.5 cm (2¾ x ⅝ in).

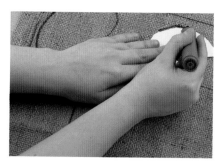

2 Leaving a 2.5 cm (1 in) hem allowance, draw a rectangle on the hessian measuring 91 x 61 cm (36 x 24 in). Transfer the design (see "Queen of Hearts"). For the border, make paisley shaped templates from card. Repeat the shapes all round the border.

4 Cut the carpet webbing tape in half, and pin to the two long edges of the hessian rectangle. Stitch in place. Using a staple gun, attach the carpet webbing tape to the frame.

6 Start by outlining the first motif. The "clippy" is worked from the back of the mat. Make a hole with the tapered end of the prodder. ▶

MATERIALS AND EQUIPMENT YOU WILL NEED

ASSORTED WOOLLEN FABRICS • TRACING PAPER • COLOURED PENCILS • HESSIAN, 96 x 66 CM (38 x 26 IN) • MARKER PEN • RULER • CARD • SCISSORS • NEEDLE AND THREAD • CARPET WEBBING TAPE, 2 M (2 YD) • WOODEN FRAME • STAPLE GUN • PRODDER • LATEX CARPET ADHESIVE AND APPLICATOR

7 Take a clipping and prod it halfway through the hessian. Place one hand underneath to catch and pull the clipping down to approximately half its length.

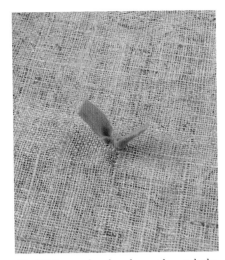

9 With your hand underneath, catch the second end of the clipping. Tug both ends down to make them even on the front of the work.

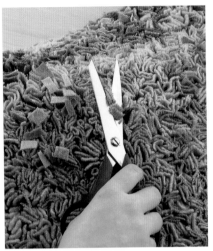

11 Remove the finished design from the frame, take off the tape and turn the rug over. Trim the work with scissors, clipping the ends to give a flat pile surface.

8 Make another hole a little less than 1 cm (½ in) away, or 4–5 warp threads of hessian. Prod in the other end of the clipping.

10 Prod the next clipping into the same hole as the end of the first clipping, and repeat. Continue over the whole design, working through the double thickness of the hem at the edges.

12 Lay the rug face down, and spread a thin layer of latex adhesive over the back. Leave to dry for 3–4 hours.

# WRAPPED JEWELLERY

THIS JEWELLERY PROJECT USES YET ANOTHER RAGWORK TECHNIQUE TO GREAT EFFECT. STRIPS OF FABRIC ARE WRAPPED ROUND A LENGTH OF WIRE, AND BOUND IN PLACE WITH COLOURED EMBROIDERY THREADS. THE FINISHED LENGTH IS THEN COILED ROUND A PEN OR PENCIL, AND SCULPTED INTO EITHER A CONE OR A LOZENGE SHAPE. MIX UNUSUAL FABRICS FOR A REALLY RICH TEXTURE, AND ADD THREADED BEADS OR SEQUINS. YOU CAN EXPERIMENT WITH OTHER SHAPES.

1 Cut the fabrics into strips 1 cm (½ in) wide and the length of the piece of wire. Starting at one end, wrap three different strips round the wire, using embroidery thread. Continue binding with the thread in sporadic patches. When you are near the end of the wire, add a loop of thick cotton thread facing the end, and continue wrapping the embroidery thread over this loop. Thread the end of the embroidery thread into the loop with one hand, and with your other hand pull the two ends of the loop to the left until the thread end is tied off.

2 Bind other coloured embroidery threads in patches along the length. Add a string of beads or sequins to give extra decoration.

3 Wrap the metallic thread round one end, then bend the end back on itself. Continue binding with the metallic thread. Finish the ends as described in step 1.

4 Wrap the finished bound length round a pen or pencil, shaping it into a spiral.

5 Remove the pen or pencil from inside the coiled length and sculpt it, working outwards and flattening it to make a cone shape. Stitch the fabric coils securely together. Stitch the brooch clip fastening to the back. Make the earrings in the same way, but form the coiled lengths into lozenge shapes instead of a cone. Stitch the earring findings to one end.

## MATERIALS AND EQUIPMENT YOU WILL NEED

WIRE, 70 CM (27½ IN) • THREE DIFFERENT FABRICS • SCISSORS •
VISCOSE OR RAYON EMBROIDERY THREADS, IN FOUR COLOURS, INCLUDING A METALLIC THREAD • THICK COTTON THREAD • BEADS OR SEQUINS •
PEN OR PENCIL • NEEDLE AND MATCHING THREAD • BROOCH CLIP FASTENING • CLIP OR FISH HOOK EARRING FINDINGS

# HOOKED HAIR ACCESSORIES

THIS SET OF HAIRSLIDE AND HAIRBOBBLES IS MADE FROM PLASTIC CARRIER BAGS AND REMNANTS OF NYLON FABRIC! IT SHOWS WHAT YOU CAN DO WITH VERY LITTLE EXPENSE. THE SAWTOOTH TEMPLATE IS EASY TO DRAW, AND YOU CAN MAKE THE WHOLE PROJECT VERY QUICKLY. WORK THE HAIRBOBBLES IN COLOURS TO MATCH THE HAIRSLIDE OR EXPERIMENT WITH DIFFERENT COLOURS, MIXING SOFT FABRIC WITH SHINY PLASTIC.

1 Make a sawtooth card template for the hairslide measuring 11 x 5 cm (4½ x 2 in). Place in the centre of the hessian and draw round it, using a marker pen. Put the hessian in the embroidery hoop.

2 Cut the red fabric and the plastic into strips 1 cm (½ in) wide. Using the fabric, begin to hook, working in rows. Outline the shape.

3 Using the plastic, hook loops to fill in the central triangles. Bring the ends of the fabric and plastic strips through to the top of the work. Trim any excess lengths.

4 Remove the hessian from the embroidery hoop. Place face down on a flat surface and cut round the shape, allowing an extra border of 2.5 cm (1 in). Apply a thin layer of latex adhesive over the back of the work and the border. Leave to dry for 3–5 minutes.

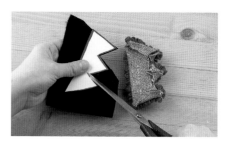

5 Turn in the edges and press down firmly. Apply small dabs of clear adhesive on the back. Lay the template on the black felt, and cut round it. Place the felt on the back of the hairslide and slip stitch in position.

6 Carefully drop a small amount of superglue on to the top surface of the hairclip fastening, then hold it in position on the back of the hairslide. Leave to dry for 1 hour before wearing. Make the hair-bobbles in the same way, using a round template of 2.5 cm (1 in) diameter. Stitch the bobbles to the elastic hairbands.

MATERIALS AND EQUIPMENT YOU WILL NEED

CARD • RULER • SCISSORS • HESSIAN, 25 x 25 CM (10 x 10 IN) • MARKER PEN • EMBROIDERY HOOP •
NYLON FABRIC • HOOK • COLOURED PLASTIC CARRIER BAGS • LATEX CARPET ADHESIVE AND APPLICATOR • CLEAR-DRYING IMPACT ADHESIVE •
BLACK FELT, 12 x 6 CM (4¾ x 2½ IN) • NEEDLE AND MATCHING THREAD • HAIRCLIP FASTENING • ELASTIC HAIRBANDS • SUPERGLUE

# CHIRPY CHAIR PAD

GIVE AN OLD KITCHEN CHAIR A NEW LEASE OF LIFE WITH THIS HOOKED CHAIR PAD. THE FARMYARD HEN MOTIF IS VERY TRADITIONAL, AND THE SPECKLED FEATHERS STAND OUT CHEERFULLY AGAINST THE ROYAL BLUE BACKGROUND. THE LAST FOUR ROWS OF HOOKED LOOPS MAKE A SIMPLE OLIVE GREEN BORDER, SPOTTED WITH RED. THE PAD IS FASTENED TO THE CHAIR WITH STRIPS OF FABRIC CUT FROM T-SHIRTS IN TONING COLOURS. YOU CAN MAKE THIS DESIGN TO FIT ANY SHAPE OF CHAIR. SIMPLY DRAW A TEMPLATE OF YOUR CHAIR SEAT AND CUT THE HESSIAN TO FIT IT EXACTLY.

**1** Place the sheet of paper over the seat and draw round the outline of the seat, using a marker pen. Cut out the shape.

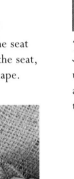

**3** Stretch the hessian on the frame, using a large-eyed needle and string. Lace up stitches through the hem of the hessian and round the frame on all sides. Keep the tension really tight.

**4** Place the paper template in the centre of the hessian and draw round the outline with a marker pen.

**2** Cut a piece of hessian the size of the chair seat, plus at least an extra 13 cm (5 in) all round. Turn under a hem, pin and then slip stitch in place.

**5** Draw a hen motif on paper. Cut out and position in the centre of the chair seat shape. Draw round the hen motif. ▶

## MATERIALS AND EQUIPMENT YOU WILL NEED

LARGE SHEET OF WHITE PAPER • MARKER PEN • SCISSORS •
PIECE OF HESSIAN, TO FIT THE SIZE OF YOUR CHAIR SEAT PLUS AT LEAST A 13 CM (5 IN) ALL ROUND •
DRESSMAKER'S PINS • NEEDLE AND STRONG THREAD • WOODEN FRAME • LARGE-EYED NEEDLE • STRING •
ASSORTED FABRICS, IN SHADES OF BROWN AND BEIGE, PLUS ROYAL BLUE, OLIVE GREEN, BLACK, RED AND WHITE • HOOK •
FOUR OLD T-SHIRTS, IN TONING COLOURS • BIAS BINDING, TO FIT THE CIRCUMFERENCE OF YOUR CHAIR PAD PLUS 5 CM (2 IN)

6 Cut the fabrics into strips 1 cm (½ in) wide. Start hooking, working the dark lines in the hen's tail and the wings first. Continue working to completely fill the hen motif.

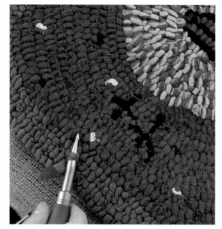

8 Work the final four rows of the pad in a contrast colour, to make a border. Add spots of bright colour at regular intervals. To make a spot, feel through the hessian and make a loop, then bring both ends of the fabric strip to the top.

10 To make ties, cut the hems off the T-shirts. Cut four strips, each approximately 38 cm (15 in) long. Fold in half and, using double thread, slip stitch one to each corner of the chair pad.

7 Begin to hook the background. Use blue or another dark colour so that the hen stands out against the background.

9 When it is completed, remove the work from the frame. Cut round the shape, allowing an extra 4 cm (1½ in) all round for a hem. Turn under the hem, pin and then slip stitch in place.

11 Pin and stitch the bias binding over the hem to neaten the underside of the chair pad. Attach the pad to the chair with the ties.

# MEDIEVAL PICTURE FRAME

THIS REGAL FRAME WAS INSPIRED BY THE STYLE OF MEDIEVAL ARCHITECTURE AND DECORATION. THE BACKED RAG WORK IS STIFF ENOUGH TO HOLD THE UNORTHODOX SHAPE EVEN WHEN IT IS HANGING ON THE WALL. THIS DESIGN HAS AN UNCUT LOOP PILE SURFACE, AND YOU CAN MAKE IT IN ANY FABRICS OR COLOURS TO SUIT YOUR ROOM. SILVER FOIL IS USED TO CREATE THE JEWELLED HIGHLIGHTS WHICH SET THE WHOLE DESIGN OFF BRILLIANTLY.

1 Draw the frame shape on the card. The shape is based on a 20 cm (8 in) square with triangles and circles added as shown. The overall size is 49 x 44 cm (19 x 17 in). Cut out the shape, then cut out a 13 cm (5 in) square in the centre. Place the template on the hessian and draw round it, using a marker pen.

2 Attach the hessian to the frame, using a staple gun. Cut the fabrics and foil into strips 1 cm (½ in) wide. Start to hook just beyond the centre square.

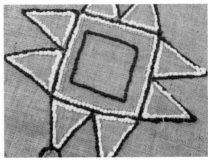

3 Outline all the shapes first, changing colour as shown. Take the fabric ends through to the top of the work. This picture shows the back view.

4 Fill in the shapes, changing colours as desired. Leave the centres of the four circles to the end.

5 Finally, fill in the centres of the circles with hooked foil strips, worked closely.

6 Remove the hessian from the frame, and lay face down on a flat surface. Cut round the shape, allowing an extra border of at least 5 cm (2 in).

▶

MATERIALS AND EQUIPMENT YOU WILL NEED

CARD, 51 x 51 CM (20 x 20 IN) • RULER • SCISSORS • HESSIAN, AT LEAST 71 x 71 CM (28 x 28 IN) • MARKER PEN • STAPLE GUN •
WOODEN FRAME • HOOK • ASSORTED FABRICS, IN FOUR COLOURS • SILVER FOIL CRISPS OR SWEETS PACKETS •
LATEX CARPET ADHESIVE AND APPLICATOR • TWO PIECES OF BLACK FELT, 51 x 51 CM (20 x 20 IN) AND 18 x 18 CM (7 x 7 CM) •
CLEAR-DRYING IMPACT ADHESIVE • DRESSMAKER'S PINS • NEEDLE AND MATCHING THREAD • RING PULL, FROM A DRINKS CAN •
PICTURE GLASS, 15 x 15 CM (6 x 6 IN)

7 Apply a thin layer of latex adhesive over the back of the work, including the central picture area and the border. Leave to dry for 3–5 minutes.

9 Cut out the large piece of black felt to fit the shape of the frame. Apply dabs of clear adhesive on the back of the work, and press on the felt. Carefully cut into the centre to reveal the picture area.

11 Use the remaining black felt to make a pocket. Pin in the centre of the back of the frame, then blanket stitch round three sides, leaving the top side open.

8 Fold in the outside border, then make diagonal cuts in the central picture area and fold back the pieces of hessian. Trim off any excess hessian. Leave to dry for 30 minutes.

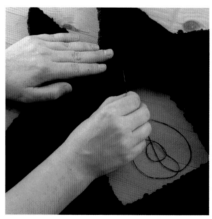

10 Slip stitch to attach the felt backing cloth securely to the back of the frame.

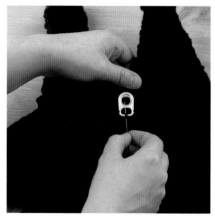

12 Stitch the ring pull in position on the back of the frame, at the centre top. Slip the picture glass into the pocket.

# TIGER SKIN RUG

MAKE THIS WILD AND WITTY RUG WITHOUT FIRING A SINGLE SHOT! IT IS, IN FACT, A VERY MODERN VERSION OF THE TRADITIONAL "CLIPPY" TECHNIQUE, USING SHORT CLIPPINGS OF WOOLLEN FABRICS TO IMITATE THE TIGER'S FUR. DON'T WORRY IF YOUR ARTISTIC SKILLS ARE NON-EXISTENT — THE CHARM OF HISTORIC RAG RUGS IS THEIR NAÏVE CHARACTER AND YOUR TIGER WILL BE UNIQUE. FORGET THE IDEA THAT RUGS HAVE TO BE RECTANGULAR OR CIRCULAR. THIS SHAPED RUG IS MADE VERY SIMPLY, USING A CARD TEMPLATE. IT IS BACKED AND FINISHED LIKE ANY OTHER RUG, AND IS AS PRACTICAL AS IT IS DECORATIVE.

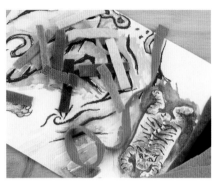

1 Draw your tiger skin design on paper. Select the woollen fabrics to match the colours you need.

3 Take one of the pieces of hessian, and pull a thread to find the straight grain of the fabric.

5 Fill in the tiger's stripes. Following the straight grain of the hessian, stretch and attach the hessian to the frame with a staple gun.

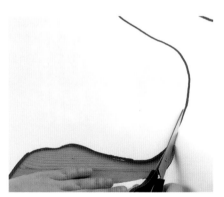

2 Make a full-size card template of the outline of the tiger skin, measuring 98 x 58 cm (38 x 23 in). Use a photocopier to enlarge your original design if necessary.

4 Lay the template on the hessian. Using a marker pen, draw round the tiger skin shape.

6 Cut all the fabrics into clippings measuring 7 x 1.5 cm (2¾ x ⅝ in).

MATERIALS AND EQUIPMENT YOU WILL NEED

DRAWING PAPER • COLOURED PENCILS • WOOLLEN FABRICS, IN SHADES OF BROWN, ORANGE, BEIGE AND CREAM, AND BLACK • CARD, 100 x 60 CM (40 x 24 IN) • SCISSORS • TWO PIECES OF HESSIAN, EACH AT LEAST 124 x 84 CM (50 x 34 IN) • MARKER PEN • WOODEN FRAME • STAPLE GUN • PRODDER • LATEX CARPET ADHESIVE AND APPLICATOR • DRESSMAKER'S PINS • NEEDLE AND MATCHING THREAD

7 Start by working the black stripes. Make a hole with the tapered end of the prodder. Take a clipping and prod it halfway through the hessian. Working with one hand underneath, catch and pull the clipping down to approximately half its length. Make another hole a little less than 1 cm (½ in) away, or 4–5 warp threads of hessian. Prod in the other end of the clipping. With your hand underneath, tug both ends of the clipping down to make them equal in length.

8 Continue prodding, working out from the centre. Fill in the design to create areas of colour and shade.

9 Turn the work over occasionally to check the front. Pull the pile to an even level.

10 When the design is completed, remove the hessian from the frame. Cut round the tiger skin shape, allowing a border of 2–3 cm (½–1¼ in).

11 Clip into the curves at regular intervals, approximately every 4 cm (1½ in). ▶

**12** Apply a thin layer of latex adhesive to the clipped border. Leave to dry for 3–5 minutes, then turn under to the back of the rug.

**14** Position the backing cloth on the back of the rug. Pin in place. Secure the backing cloth to the rug either by stitching or by applying a thin layer of latex adhesive.

**13** Take the second piece of hessian. Lay the card template on top and draw round it to make the backing cloth. Cut out, allowing an extra 2 cm ($\frac{1}{2}$ in) border all round. Fold under the raw edges, pin and tack.

**15** Turn the rug over to the right side. Clip the ends to create an even pile all over the surface.

# QUEEN OF HEARTS

THIS WONDERFULLY RICH PORTRAIT SHOWS WHAT YOU CAN DO WITH THE HOOKING TECHNIQUE. A WIDE RANGE OF DIFFERENT FABRICS AND YARNS HAS BEEN USED, INCLUDING STRIPS OF PRINTED COTTON ALONGSIDE FANCY KNITTING YARNS, SO THIS IS AN IDEAL PROJECT FOR USING UP YOUR SEWING AND KNITTING LEFTOVERS. DARK TONES ARE BALANCED BY BRIGHT PRIMARY COLOURS, AND THE GLITTERING METALLICS GIVE THE NECESSARY REGAL TOUCH. THE PORTRAIT IS HOOKED CLOSELY AND THE CONTRASTING AREAS OF CUT AND LOOP PILE CREATE A SCULPTED, ILLUSTRATIVE PICTURE.

1 Using a marker pen, draw the outline of the design on the tracing paper, based on a 41 cm (16 in) square. Colour in with the coloured pencils, as a guide for the fabrics and yarns.

2 Turn over the tracing paper and draw over all the outlines of the design, using a transfer pencil.

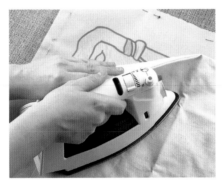

3 Pin the tracing on to the hessian, with the transfer side face down. Keeping both the tracing paper and hessian perfectly flat, cover with a pressing cloth. Iron with a hot iron until the whole image has transferred on to the hessian.

4 Remove the tracing paper and draw over the design, using the marker pen.

5 Keeping the warp and weft threads straight, attach the hessian to the frame. Staple around the frame at close intervals, every 5 cm (2 in). ▶

## MATERIALS AND EQUIPMENT YOU WILL NEED

MARKER PEN • TRACING PAPER 45 x 45 CM (18 x 18 IN) • COLOURED PENCILS • TRANSFER PENCIL • DRESSMAKER'S PINS • HESSIAN, AT LEAST 71 x 71 CM (28 x 28 IN) • IRON AND PRESSING CLOTH • STAPLE GUN • WOODEN FRAME • ASSORTMENT OF FABRICS AND YARNS, INCLUDING METALLICS • HOOK • SCISSORS • NEEDLE AND STRONG THREAD • LATEX CARPET ADHESIVE AND APPLICATOR • CARPET WEBBING TAPE, 2 M (2 YD) (OPTIONAL)

**6** Using the design as a guide, begin to match colours. Prepare the fabrics by cutting them into strips approximately 1 cm (½ in) wide.

**7** Start to hook, pulling up the loops to a height of 5 mm (¼ in). It does not matter where you begin.

**8** Hook very closely, leaving only 1–2 warp threads of hessian between each loop. When you are working with yarn you may need to hook loops through the same space twice to create a denser pile.

**9** You may find it more interesting to move from one area to another. Create subtle tones and textural changes by shearing some of the loops. Once you have a dense enough pile, use your scissors to sculpt the surface. Continue until the whole design has been hooked. Remove the hessian from the frame.

**10** Trim round the design, allowing a border of approximately 5 cm (2 in). Turn under the hem, snipping the fabric at intervals to make it lie flat. Pin in position, then tack around the border on all four sides.

**11** Lay the work face down on a flat surface. Spread a thin layer of latex adhesive over the back and leave to dry for 3 hours. If wished, cover the hessian hem with carpet webbing tape to neaten.

# PLAITED SPIRAL RUG

PLAITING, OR BRAIDING, IS ONE OF THE MOST SIMPLE RAG RUG TECHNIQUES, REQUIRING NO SPECIAL EQUIPMENT. CHANGE THE COLOURS AS YOU WORK, ALTERNATING LIGHT AND DARK FABRICS OR SUBTLY MERGING ONE COLOUR INTO THE NEXT. YOU CAN ALSO EXPERIMENT WITH PLAIN PRIMARY COLOURS FOR A BOLD EFFECT, OR USE TWEED OR TARTAN FABRICS FOR MORE SUBTLE COLOUR VARIATIONS. PLAITING IS A VERY TRADITIONAL TECHNIQUE, AND AS WELL AS BEING APPLIED TO WHOLE RUGS, IT WAS FREQUENTLY USED TO CREATE A SIMPLE BORDER ROUND A DECORATIVE HOOKED DESIGN.

1 Cut or tear the fabrics into strips 5 cm (2 in) wide. Hand stitch the strips end to end, with right sides facing. Make three long strips, each measuring 100 cm (40 in).

2 Fasten the ends of the three strips together with a safety pin. Hook the safety pin over a cuphook screwed securely into a flat surface (a wall is ideal), just above eye level.

3 Start plaiting near the safety pin. Bring the righthand strip over the middle strip, then the lefthand strip over the new middle strip. Continue plaiting, turning the raw edges under as much as possible, until you have about 20 cm (8 in) of fabric left unplaited. Secure the loose ends with a pin. Remove the safety pin and taper the beginning of the plait, trimming as necessary. Stitch neatly to conceal the raw edges.

▶

## MATERIALS AND EQUIPMENT YOU WILL NEED

AT LEAST EIGHT ASSORTED FABRICS OF SIMILAR WEIGHT – COTTON PRINT DRESS FABRICS WERE USED HERE • SCISSORS • DRESSMAKER'S PINS • NEEDLE AND MATCHING THREADS • SAFETY PIN • CUPHOOK • BACKING FABRIC, 79 X 79 CM (31 X 31 IN)

4 Using the tapered point as the centre, start winding the plait around it in a spiral. Stitch it together as you go, using double thread. Stitch right through the plait at the beginning of the spiral to attach the fabrics firmly together. Work with the spiral flat on a table and do not pull the thread too tight, otherwise the rug will not be flat.

5 Stitch first through a section of one plait, then through a section of the adjacent plait, so that the stitches do not show. Every 7 cm (2¾ in), pass the needle right through the plait and back again to secure it to the spiral.

6 When you get near the end of the plait, add more strips of fabric and then plait them. In this way, you can change colours as the rug grows.

7 When the rug reaches 73 cm (28½ in) diameter, taper the strips for the last 20 cm (8 in). Plait, then stitch a tapered point as at the beginning. Stitch neatly against the rug, as shown.

8 Place the rug on the backing fabric. Cut around the rug shape, leaving an extra 2 cm (¾ in). Lay the rug face down and pin the backing fabric on the back, turning the extra 2 cm (¾ in) under. Back stitch across the backing fabric, working from the centre outwards in an asterisk pattern.

9 Stitch the backing cloth to the edge of the rug, using small, neat stitches.

# CHILD'S SCALLOPED RUG

THE MACHINE-STITCHED EDGING GIVES THIS BEAUTIFUL RUG A VERY UNUSUAL SHAPE. WHEN YOU ARE SELECTING THE FABRICS FOR THE SCALLOPS, CHOOSE BRIGHT COLOURS AND DIFFERENT TEXTURES TO MAKE THEM A REAL FEATURE. THE ABSTRACT DESIGN INCLUDES PURPLES, REDS, SEA BLUE, GOLD AND RICH SHADES OF GREEN, SET AGAINST THE PROMINENT SWIRLING BLACK LINES. HEAVY AND LIGHTWEIGHT FABRICS ARE MIXED TO CREATE A RICH TEXTURE, WITH NATURAL YARNS ALONGSIDE NYLON FABRICS. THIS IS A MAGIC CARPET THAT CHILDREN OF ALL AGES WILL NEVER GROW TIRED OF!

**1** Draw your design on paper, and colour it in. Select a variety of fabrics to match the colours in the design.

**3** To make a card template for the scallop edging, divide the short side of the rectangle by the number of scallops required, and add 1 cm (½ in) seam allowance. Cut out each scallop from a double thickness of fabric.

**5** Place the scallops along the short sides of the hessian, with the straight sides extending 1 cm (½ in) beyond the marked rectangle. Machine stitch.

**2** Using a marker pen and ruler, draw a rectangle on the hessian measuring 100 x 50 cm (40 x 20 in). Leave an extra border of at least 13 cm (5 in) all round. Draw your design within the rectangle.

**4** Place each pair of scallops wrong sides together. Machine stitch, leaving a 1 cm (½ in) seam allowance and leaving the straight sides open. Turn the scallops right side out and press.

**6** Attach the hessian to the frame. If you are using an assortment of fabrics of different weights, cut the thicker fabrics in narrower strips than the thinner fabrics. ▶

## MATERIALS AND EQUIPMENT YOU WILL NEED

DRAWING PAPER • COLOURED PENCILS • ASSORTED FABRICS, IN BRIGHT COLOURS • MARKER PEN • RULER •
HESSIAN, AT LEAST 126 x 76 CM (50 x 30 IN) • CARD • SCISSORS • SEWING MACHINE • IRON • WOODEN FRAME • STAPLE GUN •
LATEX CARPET ADHESIVE AND APPLICATOR • FELT, 100 x 50 CM (40 x 20 IN) • DRESSMAKER'S PINS • CARPET BINDING TAPE, 3.5 M (3½ YD)

7 Begin hooking in the centre of the design. Change colour when desired.

8 Continue filling in areas of colour. Note how the black provides a strong contrast to the other colours.

9 Hook the background. To blend two colours, hook with two different coloured strips at once, pulling up long loops and then trimming down to make an even pile.

10 When the whole rug is hooked, you can add accents in brighter fabrics and yarns.

11 Remove the rug from the frame, and place face down on a flat surface. Tuck the scallops under the rug to protect them. Cover the back of the rug with latex adhesive, including the border. Leave to dry for 3–5 minutes, then fold in the border. Leave to dry for 1–2 hours.

12 Place the felt on the back of the rug and stitch in position. Pin the carpet binding tape to the edges of the rug and slip stitch.

# MYTHOLOGICAL BEAST

TRADITIONAL RAG RUGS OFTEN DEPICTED A FARMYARD ANIMAL OR A LION AS THE CENTRAL MOTIF. THIS WONDERFUL CREATURE CONJURES UP IMAGES OF EARLY CAVE PAINTINGS, MINOAN FORMS OR EVEN A WOOLLY MAMMOTH. THERE IS A MIXTURE OF LOOP AND CUT PILE, AND THE LOOPS ARE CUT TO DIFFERENT LENGTHS, CREATING A VERY RICH AND COMPLEX TEXTURE. UNSPUN FLEECE, MOHAIR AND NOVELTY KNITTING YARNS ALL ADD TO THE EFFECT.

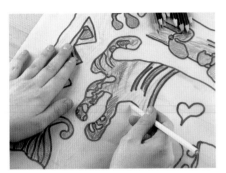

**1** Using a marker pen, draw the design on tracing paper based on a rectangle measuring 32 x 41 cm (12½ x 16 in). Colour it in.

**2** Reverse the tracing paper and, using the transfer pencil, draw over the outline and details of the design.

**3** Pin the traced design on to the hessian, with the transfer side face down. Keeping both the tracing paper and the hessian perfectly flat, cover with a pressing cloth and go over the design with a hot iron until the whole image has transferred on to the hessian.

**4** Remove the tracing paper and draw over the design with the marker pen. Attach the hessian to the frame. Using your original design as a guide, match the colours with the fabrics and yarns. Cut the fabric into strips 1 cm (½ in) wide.

**5** Start hooking, pulling the loops to a height of 5 mm (¼ in). It does not matter where you begin as this approach is very much like painting a picture.

▶

## MATERIALS AND EQUIPMENT YOU WILL NEED

MARKER PEN • TRACING PAPER, 45 x 45 CM (18 x 18 IN) • COLOURED PENCILS • TRANSFER PENCIL • DRESSMAKER'S PINS • PRESSING CLOTH • IRON • HESSIAN, AT LEAST 66 x 66 CM (26 x 26 IN) • STAPLE GUN • WOODEN FRAME • ASSORTED FABRICS • ASSORTED KNITTING YARNS, INCLUDING NOVELTY YARNS AND UNSPUN FLEECE • HOOK • SCISSORS • NEEDLE AND STRONG THREAD • LATEX CARPET ADHESIVE AND APPLICATOR • CARPET WEBBING TAPE, 2 M (2 YD) (OPTIONAL)

**6** Hook the beast in vertical rows, leaving some of the loops longer to give more texture. Use a variety of tones and blend fabrics and novelty yarns to enhance the body shape.

**8** Work the background, hooking loops very closely up against the outline of the beast. Combine cut and uncut loops to create a varied texture.

**10** Remove the work from the frame. Trim round the design, allowing a border of approximately 4 cm (1½ in). Turn the border under, snipping it at intervals so that the fabric lies flat. Pin, then tack round the piece.

**7** The silver and gold heart is trimmed a little shorter than the surrounding loops, as is the beast's eye. The eye is hooked in black-and-white knitting wool.

**9** In the background, hook a mixture of fabrics, including unspun fleece, mohair and novelty yarns. Cut the hooked fleece so that it spreads out. Leave some of the loops of novelty yarn longer for textural interest.

**11** Lay the work face down on a flat surface. Spread a thin layer of latex adhesive over the back. Leave to dry for 3 hours. If wished, cover the hessian hem with carpet webbing tape to neaten.

# POLKA DOT TEACOSY

Brighten up your tea table with this cheerful design, made from old T-shirts. The teacosy is lined with an extra layer of felt in a matching bright colour, so it will really keep the teapot warm. The sides are fastened with ribbon ties, which contrast with the chunky loop pile texture of the rag work. Bold colours work best for this simple two-colour design. The dotty eggcosies are made following the same instructions, but the sides are stitched together all the way down instead of using ribbon ties.

1 Attach one piece of hessian to the frame, using a staple gun. Make a card template of the teacosy shape, 21 cm (8¼ in) wide x 23 cm (9 in) high, including the curved top and round handle. Place the template in the centre of the hessian and draw round it, using a marker pen. Draw in some large random spots freehand. Cut the fabrics into strips 1 cm (½ in) wide. Begin hooking from the centre outwards, making loops approximately 5 mm (¼ in) high. Work the spots in purple and the background in turquoise. When completed, remove the work from the frame. Make the back of the teacosy in the same way.

2 Place the teacosy shapes face down on a flat surface and cut round them, leaving a border of at least 4 cm (1½ in). Fold under the edges and slip stitch.

3 To make the side ties, cut the ribbon into four equal lengths of 10 cm (4 in). Attach the ties to the bottom edges of both teacosy shapes, stitching the ribbon to the inside.

4 Using the template, cut out two teacosy shapes from the felt. Place one on the back of each hooked shape. Using the matching embroidery thread, blanket stitch round the edge.

5 Place the two teacosy shapes wrong sides together. Using the embroidery thread, stitch them securely together along the top curved edge. Leave the sides open to fasten with the ribbon ties.

## MATERIALS AND EQUIPMENT YOU WILL NEED

Two pieces of hessian, each at least 30 x 30 cm (12 x 12 in) • Staple gun • Wooden frame • Card • Marker pen • Turquoise and purple cotton T-shirt fabrics • Hook • Scissors • Needle and thread • Turquoise embroidery thread • Turquoise ribbon, 5 x 40 cm (2 x 16 in) • Two pieces of turquoise felt, each 30 x 30 cm (12 x 12 in)

# DOMINO HAIRSLIDE AND EARRINGS

THIS MATCHING SET IS VERY QUICK AND EASY TO MAKE, USING AN EMBROIDERY HOOP. THE CONTRAST SPOTS STAND OUT IN LOOPS AGAINST THE CUT PILE BACKGROUND, CREATING A VERY EFFECTIVE DOMINO DESIGN. THE HAIRSLIDE AND CLIP-ON EARRINGS WOULD MAKE A FUN PRESENT FOR A FASHION-CONSCIOUS CHILD. COTTON JERSEY FABRICS ARE IDEAL FOR THIS PROJECT, BUT YOU COULD USE ANY PLAIN-COLOURED FABRICS IN STRONGLY CONTRASTING COLOURS.

1 Make a card template measuring 10 x 4 cm (4 x 1½ in). Place it in the middle of the piece of hessian, and draw round it, using a marker pen. Place the hessian in the embroidery hoop. Cut the fabric into strips 1 cm (½ in) wide. Begin hooking one of the colour blocks, working from the outside edge towards the centre.

2 Shear off the tops of the loops to create a cut pile surface. Repeat to make the second block of colour.

3 For the spots, hook small loops in the contrasting colours. Do not cut these loops. Trim the excess fabric ends.

4 Remove the work from the hoop and place face down on a flat surface. Cut around the shape, allowing an extra border of 2 cm (¾ in) all round. Apply a thin layer of latex adhesive over the back of the work and the border. Leave to dry for 3–5 minutes. Turn in the border edges, and press down firmly.

5 Apply small dabs of clear adhesive on the back of the hairslide, then cover with the black felt. Slip stitch round the edge of the hairslide. Carefully drop a small amount of superglue on the hairclip fastening, then press it on to the back of the hairslide. Leave to dry for 1 hour. Make the earrings the same way, using a 2.5 cm (1 in) square template or a circle of the same size. Glue the earring findings to the back.

## MATERIALS AND EQUIPMENT YOU WILL NEED

CARD • RULER • HESSIAN, 30 x 30 CM (12 x 12 IN) • MARKER PEN • EMBROIDERY HOOP • COTTON JERSEY FABRIC, IN TWO CONTRASTING COLOURS • HOOK • SCISSORS • LATEX CARPET ADHESIVE AND APPLICATOR • CLEAR-DRYING IMPACT ADHESIVE • BLACK FELT, 10 x 4 CM (4 x 1½ IN) • NEEDLE AND MATCHING THREAD • HAIRCLIP FASTENING • CLIP EARRING FINDINGS • SUPERGLUE

# HALF-MOON HEARTHRUG

A SEMI-CIRCULAR SHAPE IS IDEAL FOR A HEARTHRUG, AND IT MAKES AN INTERESTING DESIGN CHALLENGE AFTER RECTANGLES AND CIRCLES. THIS DESIGN IS HALF OF A GIANT FLOWER, WITH DIFFERENT PATTERNS USED TO FILL IN EACH PETAL. A LINE OF STRONG RED OUTLINES THE SHAPES, AND COORDINATES WITH THE MANY OTHER COLOURS USED IN THE DESIGN. THE FREEHAND DRAWING OF THE PETALS AND THE CUT PILE SURFACE CREATE A PAINTERLY EFFECT, AND THE BRIGHT COLOURS ARE VERY CHEERFUL. THIS IS A RUG YOU WILL ENJOY SITTING BY IN WINTER OR SUMMER!

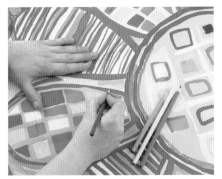

1 Sketch the outline of your design on drawing paper. Fill in with coloured pencils. Use this as a colour guide for matching the fabrics.

3 With the aid of the rotary cutter and a ruler, lay the fabrics on the cutting mat and cut strips approximately 1 cm (½ in) wide and a good length.

5 Continue hooking, working outwards and changing colour when desired.

2 Using a marker pen, draw the design on the hessian, allowing an extra border of at least 13 cm (5 in) all round. Using a staple gun, attach the hessian to the frame.

4 Begin hooking the design, forming rows of close loops. Follow your paper drawing as a guide. Start at the straight edge of the half-moon shape.

6 Check the back of your work as you proceed. Bring the ends of the fabric strips through to the top.

▶

## MATERIALS AND EQUIPMENT YOU WILL NEED

DRAWING PAPER • COLOURED PENCILS • MARKER PEN • TWO PIECES OF HESSIAN, EACH THE SIZE OF YOUR DESIGN PLUS AT LEAST 13 CM (5 IN) ALL ROUND • STAPLE GUN • WOODEN FRAME • ASSORTED FABRICS, IN VARIOUS TONES OF YELLOW, RED, BLUE, ORANGE AND CREAM • ROTARY CUTTER • RULER • CUTTING MAT • HOOK • SCISSORS • LATEX CARPET ADHESIVE AND APPLICATOR

7 Shear across the top of the loops to create a cut pile surface. This gives a more painterly effect. Continue hooking until all areas of the design are filled in.

8 Remove the rug from the frame and lay face down on a flat surface. Cut away the surplus hessian to leave a border of 8 cm (3 in).

9 Place the second piece of hessian on the back of the rug. Feeling the half-moon rug shape with your hand, use the marker pen to draw round it. Cut out the shape and put on one side.

10 Apply a thin layer of latex adhesive over the back of the rug. Leave to dry for 3–5 minutes.

11 Using the second piece of hessian as backing fabric, lay it on the latexed back of the rug. Press and smooth flat.

12 Using scissors, snip the hessian border at intervals. Apply a thin layer of latex adhesive to the snipped border and press down firmly on to the backing. Leave to dry overnight.

# STRAWBERRY CUSHION

CHOOSE BRIGHT, EVEN ACIDIC, COLOURS TO GIVE THIS CONTEMPORARY DESIGN A REAL BITE. THE YELLOW PIPING MAKES A BEAUTIFUL FINISH, AND THE INNER COVER CAN BE FILLED WITH FABRIC OFFCUTS FROM YOUR RAGWORK PROJECTS. THE BACK OF THE CUSHION CAN EITHER BE HOOKED IN THE SAME DESIGN OR LEFT PLAIN. YOU COULD DESIGN OTHER FRUIT CUSHIONS TO GO WITH THIS ONE — TRY A BUNCH OF GRAPES OR A PINEAPPLE.

1 Attach one piece of hessian to the frame, using a staple gun. Draw a square 40 x 40 cm (16 x 16 in) with a marker pen. Draw a simple strawberry shape inside the square, as shown.

2 Cut the fabrics into strips 4 cm (1½ in) wide. Begin hooking in the centre of the strawberry. When you have filled in a small area, shear off the loops to create a cut pile surface. Complete the design.

3 Remove the hessian from the frame. Repeat for the back of the cushion cover, or hook a plain back. Lay both squares face down on a flat surface, and cut round them, allowing an extra border of 10 cm (4 in) all round. Fold under a hem and slip stitch.

4 Wrap the strip of yellow fabric round the piping cord. Machine stitch along the length close to the cord.

5 Place the front cushion cover face down on a flat surface. Pin the piping cord as close to the edge as possible. Hand stitch, using small tacking stitches.

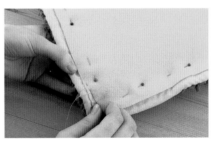

6 Take one piece of felt, and pin in position on the reverse side of the front cushion cover. Stitch round the shape, using running stitch. Repeat to attach the second piece of felt to the reverse of the back cushion cover.

▶

MATERIALS AND EQUIPMENT YOU WILL NEED

TWO PIECES OF HESSIAN, EACH AT LEAST 66 x 66 CM (26 x 26 IN) • WOODEN FRAME • STAPLE GUN • RULER • MARKER PEN • ASSORTED FABRICS, IN RED, BLUE, YELLOW AND GREENS • HOOK • SCISSORS • NEEDLE • SEWING THREADS: WHITE, YELLOW AND BLACK • YELLOW COTTON FABRIC, 170 x 7 CM (65 x 3 IN), CUT ON THE BIAS AND JOINED AS NECESSARY • PIPING CORD, 170 CM (65 IN) • SEWING MACHINE • DRESSMAKER'S PINS • TWO PIECES OF YELLOW FELT, EACH 40 x 40 CM (16 x 16 IN) • SIX PRESS STUDS • TWO PIECES OF CALICO, EACH 42 x 42 CM (16½ x 16½ IN) • FABRIC CLIPPINGS, OR CUSHION PAD

84
STRAWBERRY CUSHION

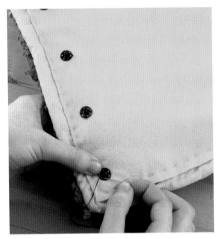

7 Space the press stud fronts 5 cm (2 in) apart along one edge of the front cushion cover. Stitch, using black thread. Stitch the corresponding backs on to the back cushion cover to match.

9 To make the inner cushion pad, place the two pieces of calico right sides together. Machine stitch round all four sides, leaving a gap of 15 cm (6 in) in one side for filling.

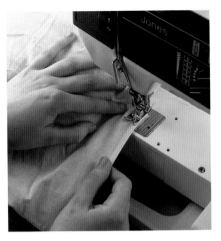

11 Using the sewing machine, stitch the two sides of the inner cover together to close the opening.

8 Place the front and the back cushion covers with wrong sides together. Using yellow thread, stitch through both sides, following the cushion's shape. Leave the side with the press studs open.

10 Turn the calico inner cover right side out. Fill it with fabric clippings. Alternatively, use a cushion pad cut to size.

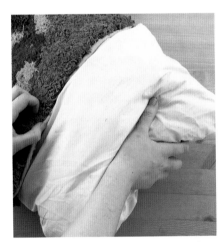

12 Place the filled inner cover inside the cushion cover. Use the press studs to close the cover.

# HOOKED HAT

THIS WONDERFUL HAT HAS EVERYTHING — A HOOKED LOOP PILE BAND DECORATED WITH MOTIFS, A MACHINE-EMBROIDERED SILK TOP, STRIPED PIPING AND A LUSCIOUS SILK LINING. IT LOOKS EQUALLY GOOD IN HOT PINKS OR AUTUMNAL COLOURS, OR YOU CAN DESIGN YOUR OWN COLOUR SCHEME. THE HAT CAN BE MADE TO FIT INDIVIDUAL SIZES, CHILD OR ADULT. AND, OF COURSE, A LINED RAGWORK HAT IS VERY WARM ON A COLD WINTER'S DAY!

**1** Measure the circumference of the head just above the ear and add 5 cm (2 in), to give the length of the hatband. The height of the hatband is 8 cm (3 in). Draw out these measurements on the hessian with a marker pen.

**2** Draw a freehand design within the hatband shape. Simple flower, leaf and heart motifs, are used here. Mark the hatband into sections.

**3** For the piping, cut two strips of striped fabric on the bias, the length of the hatband plus 3 cm (1¼ in) x 6 cm (2½ in), including the seam allowances. A rotary cutter is useful for this. With wrong sides together, stitch along the length of one strip with a 1 cm (½ in) seam allowance for the bottom piping. The top piece of piping has two seams. Stitch the striped fabric to the lining fabric along the long edges, with wrong sides together, leaving 1 cm (½ in) seam allowances. Stuff the piping with cord or a strip of old blanket.

**4** Attach the hessian to the frame, using the staple gun. Stitch the right side of the bottom piping to the hessian, along the lower edge of the hatband. Stitch the piping with the two seams at the top of the hatband as shown.

**5** Prepare the fabrics for hooking the hat band. Cut them into strips of 1 cm (2½ in) wide, varying the width according to the weight of fabric.

### MATERIALS AND EQUIPMENT YOU WILL NEED

TAPE MEASURE • HESSIAN, THE SIZE OF THE HATBAND PLUS AT LEAST 8 CM (3 IN) ALL ROUND • MARKER PEN • RULER • ROTARY CUTTER • CUTTING MAT • FOUR FABRICS: STRIPED, COLOURED LINING, COLOURED FELT AND COLOURED SILK, EACH 50 x 50 CM (20 x 20 IN) • ASSORTED FABRICS, FOR HOOKING • CORD OR OLD BLANKET FABRIC • WOODEN FRAME • STAPLE GUN • NEEDLE AND MATCHING THREADS • SCISSORS • LATEX CARPET ADHESIVE AND APPLICATOR • DRESSMAKER'S PINS • STRONG THREAD • PAPER • PENCIL • DRAWING PIN • SEWING MACHINE • LUREX SEWING THREAD

6 Begin hooking the design, working close loops. Change the background colour between sections as shown.

7 When the hatband is complete, remove the hessian from the frame. Cut round the hooked hatband, allowing an extra border of 4 cm (1½ in).

8 Spread latex adhesive over the back of the hooking, and leave to dry for 3–5 minutes, then turn back the hem. Leave the side edges open.

9 Pin the side edges of the hatband together. Using strong thread, stitch the seam together closely. The stitches will be hidden by the loop pile surface.

10 Make a paper pattern for the top of the hat. Take the length of the hatband plus 2 cm (¾ in), and divide by 6.3. Add an extra 1 cm (½ in) seam allowance. Draw a circle on paper, using a tape measure secured by a drawing pin at one end and a pencil held at the desired measurement. Using this as a template, cut two layers of silk and one of felt.

11 Machine embroider the layers of fabric together, with the felt uppermost. Using zigzag stitch and a lurex thread in the bobbin of the machine, stitch circles. Slice the silk between the stitching and fray the edges for a decorative finish. ▶

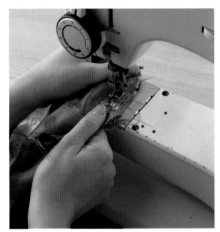

**12** Cut out a silk lining band to the same measurements as the original hatband. Pin to the hat top lining and machine stitch round the edge.

**14** Neatly stitch the lining inside the hat, turning under the seam allowance.

**13** With right sides together, pin the top of the hat to the hatband. Hand stitch together.

# TEXTURED SHOULDER BAG

RAGWORK CAN BE COMBINED WITH OTHER TEXTILE TECHNIQUES, SUCH AS APPLIQUÉ OR PATCHWORK, TO GIVE A RICHLY TEXTURED SURFACE. IN THIS DESIGN, FLAT PIECES OF PATTERNED FABRICS ARE APPLIQUÉD TO PADDED HESSIAN, AND THEN SURROUNDED BY HOOKED LOOPS. CHOOSE FABRICS WITH UNUSUAL PATTERNS AND UNCONVENTIONAL COLOUR COMBINATIONS. FINALLY THE BAG IS DECORATED WITH CORD AND TASSELS. TO COMPLETE THE RICH EFFECT, USE A BRIGHTLY COLOURED OR PATTERNED FABRIC FOR THE BACK, AND A CONTRAST FABRIC FOR THE LINING.

1 Draw a rectangle on the hessian measuring 25 x 18 cm (10 x 7 in), using a marker pen. Draw your design inside this. Tack the blanket to areas of the hessian, as padding for the appliqué. Choose appliqué fabrics and stitch in place, turning under the raw edges.

3 Cut three pieces of lining fabric the same size as the hooked panel, plus a seam allowance all round. Place two pieces right sides together. Machine stitch round, leaving one short side open.

5 Stitch the cord along both long sides of the bag, extending it in a loop at the top for carrying. Stitch the tassels to the bottom corners, concealing the ends of the cord.

2 Using the staple gun, attach the hessian to the frame. Begin hooking round the appliqué shapes, using a rich mixture of fabrics. Continue until the design is completed, then remove the hessian from the frame.

4 Cut out the hooked panel, allowing an extra 2 cm (¾ in) border all round. Apply a thin layer of latex adhesive over the back, then turn under the border. With wrong sides together, hand stitch the third piece of lining fabric to the panel, turning in the seam allowance and leaving the top edge open.

6 Place the inner lining inside the bag, wrong sides together. Stitch round the top edge, turning under the raw edge of the lining. Stitch the press stud to the centre top edges of the bag, with one half on each side.

## MATERIALS AND EQUIPMENT YOU WILL NEED

HESSIAN, AT LEAST 46 x 46 CM (18 x 18 IN) • MARKER PEN • RULER • PIECE OF OLD BLANKET • NEEDLE AND THREAD •
ASSORTED FABRICS, FOR THE HOOKING AND THE APPLIQUÉ • STAPLE GUN • WOODEN FRAME • HOOK • SEWING MACHINE •
LINING FABRIC, 92 x 92 CM (36 x 36 IN) • LATEX CARPET ADHESIVE AND APPLICATOR • CORD, 1.5 M (1½ YD) • TWO TASSELS • PRESS STUD

# PLASTIC BATHMAT

A T LAST, A USE FOR UNWANTED PLASTIC CARRIER BAGS! THEY ARE, OF COURSE, WATERPROOF AND SO MAKE AN IDEAL AND VERY COLOURFUL BATHMAT. THE CHECKERBOARD DESIGN IS DRAWN OUT FIRST ON GRAPH PAPER. THE SQUARES OF THE GRAPH PAPER CORRESPOND TO THE HOLES IN THE CANVAS, WHICH IS USED IN THIS PROJECT INSTEAD OF HESSIAN AS IT GIVES RIGIDITY TO THE FINISHED MAT AND MAKES IT EASIER TO WORK IN STRAIGHT LINES. SHOP AROUND TO COLLECT PLASTIC BAGS IN DIFFERENT TONES FOR A REALLY SUBTLE EFFECT — RECYCLING HAS NEVER BEEN SO CREATIVE.

1 Sketch the design on graph paper. Using coloured pencils, fill in the blocks of colour.

2 Sort the plastic bags to colour-match the design. Cut the plastic into strips 2 cm (¾ in) wide.

3 Using a marker pen and ruler, draw a rectangle 69 x 38 cm (27 x 15 in) on the canvas. Allow for an extra border four holes deep all round.

4 Cut out the canvas rectangle. Stick masking tape along the two short edges. Fold under the top and bottom borders. You may find it helpful to G-clamp the canvas to a tabletop.

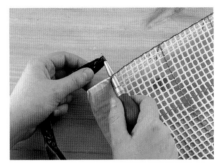

5 Begin in the top lefthand corner, hooking through the double layer of canvas. Hold the plastic strip with one hand under the canvas, and with your other hand push the hook through the first hole. Feed the end of the plastic strip on to the hook, and pull it up to the top.

6 Push the hook into the next hole, and pull through the first loop to a height of 2 cm (¾ in). ▶

MATERIALS AND EQUIPMENT YOU WILL NEED

GRAPH PAPER • COLOURED PENCILS • PLASTIC BAGS, IN VARIOUS TONES OF YELLOW, WHITE, BLUE AND GREEN • MARKER PEN • RULER • SCISSORS • OPEN-WEAVE RUG CANVAS (THREE HOLES PER 2.5 CM/1 IN), 84 x 56 CM (33½ x 22 IN) • MASKING TAPE • G-CLAMP (OPTIONAL) • HOOK • NEEDLE AND STRONG THREAD • DRESSMAKER'S PINS • INVISIBLE THREAD • WATERPROOF FABRIC BACKING CLOTH, 71 x 40 CM (28 x 16 IN)

7 Continue to fill in the grid lines. Work a single row round the edge of the mat, and a double row for all the other grid lines.

9 Check the back of the work to make sure that all the strip ends have been pulled through to the top of the mat. Trim off any excess lengths of plastic.

11 Place the waterproof backing cloth on the back of the design, turning under the edges on all four sides. Pin the backing cloth to the canvas.

8 When all the grid lines are complete, start to fill in the squares. Work the loops in rows.

10 Lay the design face down on a flat surface. Remove the masking tape. Using a strong thread, stitch the hems.

12 Using invisible thread, blanket stitch round the bathmat to secure the backing cloth.

# SUPPLIERS

**United Kingdom**

Alec Tiranti Ltd
(Mail order)
70 High Street
Theale
Reading
Berkshire RG7 5AR
*Latex adhesive*

Creativity
(Mail order available)
45 New Oxford Street
London WC1A 1BH
*Tapestry canvas, hessian and
embroidery hoops*

Lynne Stein
(Mail order)
4 Oakdale Court
Grey Road
Altrincham
Cheshire WA14 4BX
*Prodders and specialist frames*

Jenni Stuart-Anderson
(Mail order)
The Birches
Middleton-on-the-Hill
Herefordshire HR6 0HZ
*Specialist tools and frames*

Lizzie Reakes
(Mail order)
68 Oaklands Road
Hanwell
London W7 2DU
*Hooks, hessian and worksheets*

Russell & Chapple Ltd
23 Monmouth Street
Shaftesbury Avenue
London WC2H 9DE
*Artist's stretchers*

Hobby Horse
15–17 Langton Street
London SW10 0JL
*Jewellery findings*

Whaleys (Bradford) Ltd
(Mail order)
Harris Court
Great Horton
Bradford
West Yorkshire BD7 4EQ
*Hessian and calico*

**Canada**

Lee Valley
5511 – Steeles Avenue
Westbin
Toronto, Ont
Tel: 416-746-0850
*Tools*

Images Art & Frames
9616 – Cameron Street
Burnaby, B.C.
Tel: 604-421-6663
*Frames*

Homecraft Importers
2348 W 4th Avenue
Vancouver, B.C.
Tel: 604-738-2614
*Felt, canvas, hessian and hoops*

**Australia**

Spotlight
60 stores throughout Australia
Tel: 1800 500 021

Artmat P/L
107 Queens Avenue
Hawthorn 3122
Tel: (03) 9818 2133
*Hessian, calico, hooks and latex*

Nancraft – Boronia Arts and
Crafts
247 Dorset Road
Boronia 3155
Tel: (03) 9762 1751
*Frames and hooks*

# ACKNOWLEDGEMENTS

The author would like to thank the following:

A big thank you to all the makers who kindly gave their time and inspiration to create stunning, beautiful work for the individual project themes: Sarah Best *(Polka Dot Teacosy and Strawberry Cushion)*; Lucinda Ganderton *(Crochet Duffel Bag and Knitted Patchwork Rug)*; Angela Harrison *(Wrapped Jewellery)*; Liz Kitchin *(Rectangular Flower Rug and Chirpy Chair Pad)*; Ali Rhind *(Paisley Clippy Mat and Tiger Skin Rug)*; Lynne Stein *(Queen of Hearts and Mythological Beast)*; Jenni Stuart-Anderson *(Plaited Spiral Rug)*; and Ju Ju Vail *(Child's Scalloped Rug, Hooked Hat and Textured Shoulder Bag)*.

Many thanks also to all those who lent work for inclusion in the Gallery section: Ann O'Dwyer at the Black Swan Guild; Vale Royal Borough Council and Winsford Community Arts Centre; Ben Hall; and Susan Lindsay. A special thanks to Dee Gilder for putting me in contact with Maureen Morano – thank you, Maureen, for the generous loan of examples from your rug collection.

I would also like to thank everyone who contributed in helping me with their time, knowledge and skills: Judith Simons, my editor; James Duncan for his step photography, patience and good humour; and Fanny Ward and Tim Imrie for the sensitive styling and photography of the finished pieces.

The publishers would like to thank The American Museum in Bath for the loan of images featured on pages 9, 10 and 11.

# INDEX